RACING AND ALL THAT

RACING AND ALL THAT

Stirling Moss and Mike Hailwood

Edited by John Thompson

PELHAM BOOKS
London

First published in Great Britain by
Pelham Books Ltd
44 Bedford Square
London WC1B 3DU
1980

British Library Cataloguing in Publication Data
Moss, Stirling
Racing and all that.
1. Automobile racing
2. Motorcycle racing
I. Hailwood, Mike
796.7′2′0924 GV1029

ISBN 0 7207 1276 9

Filmset by Saildean Ltd,
and printed and bound in Great Britain by
Billing & Sons Ltd, Guildford, London and Worcester

Contents

Illustrations

Between pages 80 and 81

Foreword
by Rob Walker

When I was asked to write the foreword to this book I was both honoured and delighted, because not only had Stirling and Mike been 'my' drivers but also, I like to think, they count among my very best friends.

They are both household names and represent the ultimate in their particular sport. Mike was undoubtedly the best on motorcycles and Stirling was the greatest racing driver of his era, and probably of all time. Although Stirling retired from Formula One eighteen years ago, his name is still synonymous with the fastest on four wheels in such phrases as 'Who do you think you are, Stirling Moss?'

Both have boundless natural skill and courage, although I'm sure they have known more fear than most. In times of extreme danger their bravery was fantastic. I recall when Mike rescued Clay Regazzoni from his crashed, burning car at Kyalami in 1973. Three times he dashed into fifteen-foot flames in an attempt to drag the unconscious Clay out of his car. The third time Mike succeeded but had to roll on the ground to put out flames which were burning him. I'm glad to say I was able to play a part in nominating Mike for the George Medal which he was awarded for his bravery in this affair.

But if there is one particular thing which sticks in my mind about both Stirling and Mike it is loyalty. When Stirling was driving F1 and F2 for me, he was also driving sports cars and what have you for other entrants, but he was also always completely loyal to the particular person he was driving for at the time.

The two of them are probably the most popular people in their sport that there have ever been. Stirling could not go anywhere in the world where he was not recognised – it didn't matter where we were, it was always the same. Sometimes it was frightening, as at Zeltweg in Austria after Stirling won their first race. We were besieged by about 10,000 fans and had to lock ourselves in the transporter, keeping it in low gear with the brakes full on. But even this was not enough and the crowd of Austrians pushed us a full hundred yards down the road in their enthusiasm. Eventually they had to be dispersed using fire hoses.

Mike, too, used to be mobbed whenever he arrived in Italy or Switzerland, and when he made his fantastic comeback to bike racing, winning his very first race on the Isle of Man and adding one more World Championship to the nine he already had, he doubled the already enormous crowd there. Mike's comeback is one of the most amazing accomplishments ever witnessed in the sporting world, especially when he had told me some years before, 'I will never return to bikes, they are too frightening'.

Stirling is also making a comeback and looks to be every bit as good as any of the present-day drivers. But it is harder for Stirling because he has had a long lay-off from competitive driving after a very serious accident. The cars are so different, with enormous tyres and fantastic late braking, that it must be like having to learn to drive again, although with his great talent I have no doubt he will make it. Maybe some of the competitive spirit and confidence will be lacking, because after Fangio retired Stirling always knew he was the best driver, and I really don't think he ever considered that anyone else was in the same class.

I imagine that, in their heart of hearts, Stirling and Mike don't have too much admiration for the present-day racing drivers, and probably think they don't even know the meaning of the word 'fear'. What is certain is that we could not have two greater experts to tell us about motorsport and how racing today compares with the old days.

1 Characters — where are they now?

STIRLING MOSS

When considering the many changes which have taken place in motor racing over the years I suppose most students of the sport would point first to engineering advances, to improvements in technology.

I'll be coming to the technical side and its associated problems soon enough - indeed it is in this area that Grand Prix racing has got itself into a bit of a mess. But first I want to concentrate on the human aspect, because for me it's the people of motor racing, the drivers especially, who have changed the most.

Gone are the great 'characters' of the sport and gone too, I fear, is the camaraderie which my contemporaries and I enjoyed. The whole nature of the game has shifted around, and so have the individuals within it. The result is that for all its razamatazz, all its high-powered sponsors and all its round-the-globe television coverage, modern-day racing seems to me to have lost some of its original flair. It's a great shame, but that's the way I see it.

I suppose the true 'characters' of Grand Prix racing were already thinning out by the end of my career. During my earlier years, however, such men abounded on the circuits - men like the Spanish nobleman, the Marquis de Portago, and the Anglo-American Harry Schell who combined racing with running a bar in Paris, or the wealthy British enthusiasts Duncan Hamilton and Tony Rolt, who together once won the Le Mans 24 Hours.

These were the sort of chaps who seemed larger than life, who could afford to come to a race, take part in one event, have an absolute ball and then go off and make their money - if they needed to - in other ways. But by the early sixties they were being supplanted – not done away with altogether, but overshadowed by better drivers with a more professional attitude. It wasn't that these men weren't potentially good enough to retain their Grand Prix status, it was simply that they didn't compete often enough to maintain peak form or to keep up with the latest technical developments.

During the fifties I came up against many such drivers. Indeed in the first few seasons of the World Drivers' Championship (inaugurated in 1950) most Grand Prix contestants, and certainly the British ones, occupied the status of 'rich amateur' rather than 'dedicated professional'. There were always the top names, like Juan Manuel Fangio, Giuseppe Farina, Froilan Gonzales or Luigi Villoresi, who would lead the works teams and monopolise the leader board, but the meat of the field would be provided by the private entries, those who took part for love rather than money, for excitement rather than glory. They were talented, these guys, but as time went on their devil-may-care approach was replaced by a more serious, more committed attitude. It was an attitude that I myself adopted, with some success. And yet, I still enjoyed my racing in a way that I fear today's drivers, those competing in the nineteen eighties, do not.

I was often accused of taking my racing *too* seriously, of being too introverted if you like, and my answer is that for me motor racing was not a hobby but my full-time occupation. To earn my living I had to win races – or at least put up the best possible show – and to achieve that I reckoned I had to concentrate pretty damned hard on what I was doing. And if that meant going to bed early (and alone!) the night before a race, then that's what I did.

This increase in professionalism, by which I mean an increase in the number of drivers who made their living behind the wheel of a racing car, inevitably marked a turning point in the history of Grand Prix racing. The 'old school' of competitors was usurped by drivers who took the business of racing that much less casually, men who were prepared to race hard every weekend.

Practice does tend to make perfect and so 'amateurs' like Duncan Hamilton and Tony Rolt, talented as they were, found themselves being beaten by people who had no more ability than they did, but who effectively became more proficient racing drivers purely by virtue of the number of miles they put in. Rolt and Hamilton, among others, turned their attention to sports cars and they were able to win a lot of races. But they would only be racing maybe once a month instead of every weekend.

Sports car racing, particularly long-distance, has always been less demanding than single-seater racing; one needed stamina, but one very rarely had to drive at nine-tenths the whole time. When Hamilton and Rolt won the 1953 Le Mans in a works C-type Jaguar, they started the race with monumental hang-overs! In his book, *Touch Wood,* Duncan admitted that they had anticipated being disqualified from the race due to an obscure breach of the regulations during practice. Ferrari had protested and so convinced were they that their Jaguar would be banned that the two drivers decided to drown their sorrows in the time-honoured fashion. After 'a night of steady imbibing', as Duncan put it, the pair were greeted with the news that a fine had been paid to the organisers and the C-type was back in the race. I was actually in the same team, but I knew nothing of what went on that night, nor even that the car faced dis-qualification. Suffice it to say that whereas my car suffered fuel feed problems the Rolt/Hamilton machine kept going perfectly to beat my co-driver Peter Walker and me by twenty-nine miles.

The point I am making is that whereas you could be living it up all night and still win a race like Le Mans, I don't believe anyone could do the same thing and then sweep to victory in a full-blooded Grand Prix, the effort required would simply be too great. Every top driver has discovered the hard way how difficult it is to race well when tired, even the great Fangio. He, indeed, nearly lost his life when fatigue caused him to crash at Monza, having driven half way across Europe the night before.

But when I talk of professionalism, I don't mean that any of us 'professionals' led a cloistered existence. Men like Harry Schell, Mike Hawthorn, Peter Collins and Froilan Gonzales were all madly ebullient, happy-go-lucky individuals who nevertheless went consistently well in Formula One. Schell was probably the most colourful of the lot and in truth he wasn't really as good a driver as he could have been. Every year people would write him off, then at the very last race old Harry would pull out all the stops and turn in a remarkably good performance as if to say, 'Look, I can be this good, and next year I will be!' Someone would then sign him up, but always he would slip back.

When Mike Hawthorn and I battled for the World Championship in 1958, he with Ferrari and myself driving a Vanwall, much was made of the contrast between us. I was small and dark, he was tall and fair, and while Mike was quite likely to be seen in the bar on the eve of a race, I was more likely to be tucked up in bed. The idea, I suppose, was to project Mike as the tearaway and myself as the dedicated disciplinarian. It was something both of us went along with because it was good publicity for the sport, but really a lot of it was exaggerated. Hawthorn, for instance, may have liked a pint or two of beer but he would never arrive at a circuit half drunk. After the race he would probably have a drink with the boys and there was nothing wrong in that. Personally, I didn't particularly like beer (I still don't), and I didn't join in – not because it offended my religious principles or anything like that, but because I preferred to lead a slightly less gregarious kind of existence.

I have always programmed my life fairly rigidly because that's the way I am and, psychologically, I think it helped while I was racing. I felt that if I had really tuned up for a race and I wasn't drinking or smoking much and I wasn't going out with women, then if the chips were down and it was a really hot day with everybody dropping by the wayside with fatigue, then, my God, I figured I deserved not to. That helped to keep the adrenalin flowing.

Mike, on the other hand, would say, 'Well, I don't think it matters a damn,' and get on with it. Pete Collins was a similar type, and so was Innes Ireland, although he came along a bit later. I often feel a little sorry for Innes because by the time he became successful, Hawthorn, Collins and company had gone and Grand Prix racing was full of guys a bit more like myself. Innes, I think, tended to put enjoying himself first and being a successful driver second and I believe he paid for it in terms of his career. He tended not to be taken as seriously as he deserved simply through being an uncompromising individualist who enjoyed life – and I'm pleased to say he's just the same now! He would have fitted in much easier, I feel, had he been racing five years earlier. But like Hawthorn, Innes was, on his day, virtually unbeatable.

Graham Hill was another who, in outlook, perhaps belonged to an earlier period. Graham was a very risqué type of character, always playing pranks and making jokes, usually at someone else's expense. Yet, and this is the significant part, Graham was deadly serious about the job of racing. In fact, you couldn't even speak to him before a race – he simply wouldn't communicate. He was as withdrawn and tense at that particular moment as he was gregarious and relaxed afterwards. To me, Graham, who, remember, was twice World Champion, proved an important point. He demonstrated – perhaps better than any driver before him – that it is possible for a Grand Prix driver to discipline himself, to adopt an appropriately staid mental attitude towards racing, so as to reach the top and then stay there, without projecting a dull or torpid image.

Hill was a driver who was made rather than born, which meant he had to work very hard indeed to keep himself competitive. At the same time, he was a tremendously exciting and interesting person to be with. Going as near as I can to the modern day, I can point to James Hunt as being cast in a similar mould. James, in fact, was (while he was racing) a nineteen seventies version of Mike Hawthorn – often behaving in a fairly outrageous manner but still capable of taking his motor racing very seriously indeed.

In the end James seemed to find it all too much for him and I suppose with his retirement went the last of the true 'characters' of the Grand Prix scene. The reason why, over the years, this type of driver has become rarer and rarer must have something to do with the life-style most of them are persuaded – through the modern demands of the job – to adopt. You see, although I presented a different image from folk like Hawthorn and Collins, I feel I was actually quite similar to them in basic outlook. They would joke around more than I would in public because that was the role expected of them.

Similarly I played to the gallery to the extent that I always *appeared* to take things more seriously. But privately I got on with both of them very well and the fact that they were essentially more flamboyant than I was I don't think affected their performance on the track.

Today's top drivers are not particularly flamboyant. Some are outspoken, many are genuinely nice guys and all of them are highly talented. But none, I would say, are of the Hawthorn type, let alone the Schell or de Portago type, and the reason is not hard to pinpoint. It is that being a modern Grand Prix driver is a job which occupies one virtually 365 days of the year – not a situation calculated to promote levity or outrageousness.

In contrast, the demands upon me as a driver lasted from a day or two before a race to a little bit after it had finished. The next morning, the racing was over and I could do as I pleased. Testing was infrequent. Monday morning you got paid and then your time was your own. Nowadays, the demands on a driver for his talent in the cockpit are the same, but the demands upon him as a person and a member of the team are far, far greater.

In short, the driver of the eighties has sold his soul to motor racing. We kept our souls while selling our character and our talent. Today's drivers, whether they like it or not, have people pulling at them from all directions – a sponsor this way, the man they drive for that way, the circuit owners another way, the safety commission in yet another direction. All these facets are time-consuming and none are likely to make motor racing more enjoyable or amusing, simply less interesting and more arduous.

Don't let me mislead anybody. Grand Prix racing is never in itself fun – not when you are actually driving. It's enjoyable only in a masochistic sort of way. It's fun when you pass someone and he can't keep up but it's not 'fun' in the sense that going to a dinner party might be fun. It's exhilarating, yes, it's rewarding, yes, it's pleasurable, yes. But fun it ain't, and never was. What was fun to us was the whole ambience of motor racing; we were steeped in the atmosphere of the thing and we loved it. Our real fun only stopped five minutes before the starting flag dropped and it began again immediately the race was over. I think that drivers today can still derive exhilaration and enjoyment from racing. I do not think, though, that they relax as we did either before or after - the pressure on them is too great.

I must say that if the same pressures of sponsorship and so on had been on me in the fifties, I probably would not have taken part, and I'm sure that the majority of my contemporaries would have felt the same way. Motor racing was just as dangerous then as it is now - more so if you study the accident statistics - and while we were perfectly aware of the risks involved we enjoyed it anyway. Our attitude was that one fought hard and one played hard. You did your best to win on the track and you did your best to have as much fun as possible off it. To us, it was the only way to keep some sense of proportion. Laugh if you like, but the Grand Prix stars of my era had more in common with Battle of Britain pilots than with today's racing heroes, and that, I think, is where the big difference lies.

James Hunt tried to play it 'our way' and it backfired. His former team-mate, the German driver Jochen Mass, highly popular with press and public, I think would even now like to join him in adopting that special kind of flamboyant attitude. Poor James, however, was like a fish out of water - there just wasn't a place for him amid the nervous tenseness of the modern-day sport. I'm sure that James anticipated that Grand Prix racing would be much more fun than it was. He clearly derived enormous pleasure from fighting his way up the ladder but once at the top things closed in on him. Try as he might, the 'fun' aspect was missing - which in turn meant that the danger aspect weighed all the more heavily on his mind. Suddenly - in mid-1979 - he drew up in his tracks and said to himself, 'What the hell am I doing here?'

I am sure that drivers today are much nearer the threshold of fear than I was. Not because they are more likely to get killed or injured, but because there is nothing to relieve the tension. The business side of Grand Prix racing, the constant rushing around from circuit to circuit, factory to factory, TV studio to TV studio, sponsor to sponsor, has deprived drivers of the opportunity to unwind. Nowadays there are no prize-giving ceremonies, no post-race parties, only mind-zapping schedules. So with the 'fun' aspect having been replaced by the necessity to appear here, there and everywhere, thoughts of how dangerous the whole thing is are bound to crop up more often. It surprises me not at all that more and more drivers are asking themselves the same question: 'Is it all worth it?' And if others choose to follow the lead of Hunt and Niki Lauda by executing a smart about-turn, then I shall be amazed even less.

Quite how this state of affairs has come about will be discussed in future chapters. There are many contributing factors: technology is one, safety is another and sponsorship is obviously a third. The drivers themselves are hardly without blame for allowing (and in certain ways actively encouraging) the development of a 'more for me' attitude which has hardly given them an easier time of it. I am convinced that modern-day drivers have little or no notion of how to enjoy life while still striving to win the World Championship, whereas drivers of my day knew exactly how to have a good time, and did so. Because we came from a time when money was much less and sport was much more, I think today we would have said, 'OK, we've got enough money, let's keep the fun here'. But it seems instead to have reached a point where 'fun' isn't even there, a forgotten aspect of motor racing as obsolete as six-inch wheel rims. Money appears to be the only thing anyone is interested in.

MIKE HAILWOOD

I've never had a particularly conventional attitude to life, and have always believed in getting as much enjoyment as possible out of everything I've done – and I still do!

It's not an attitude which endeared me to team bosses when I returned to Grand Prix racing in the seventies, I know. Things had certainly changed since my first forays in Formula One in the early sixties. In those days drivers really used to enjoy themselves between races, and we all got to know each other very well off the track as well as on it. I honestly never knew any of the other drivers particularly well in the seventies – there just didn't seem to be the time or the inclination to get together.

It was all very different from those early years when I was racing – or should I say, attempting to race – for the Parnell team, together with Chris Amon and Peter Revson. The three of us shared a flat with Tony Maggs in Ditton Road, Surbiton and although we didn't make much of an impression *on* the track, 'the Ditton Road Flyers' probably broke quite a few records *off* it! Bruce McLaren was living just down the road with Tyler Alexander, Eoin Young and Bruce Abernathy – another Kiwi racer – and many a night was spent carousing till dawn in a pub which will be known for ever as 'Pete's' after its cheerful owner. And I don't think that another of our favourite haunts, the Contented Plaice ever quite recovered from the night we took it over to celebrate Chris's twenty-first birthday.

We used to get ourselves into all kinds of scrapes, and I remember one particular incident vividly. Chris was very much enamoured of a certain very attractive blonde to whom he had been introduced by one 'Captain' Peter Jensen. Everything was fine until his amorous exploits were discovered by the lady's boyfriend, who just happened to be a member of the Mafia! Needless to say, we had to hide Chris away for a few days until all the fuss had died down.

I honestly don't think that any of us suffered on the track simply because we were so busy enjoying life between races. We still took the serious part seriously and I'm sure we all went just as well and as hard. Having a good time made no difference, save for keeping us happier!

Mind you, I'm not sure that anything would have made much difference to the performances of Chris, Revvie and myself! The Parnell equipe, under the watchful eye of Big Tim, was not exactly renowned for its preparation. In fact it became a standard joke on a Monday morning that Tim, just returned from the weekend on his Derbyshire pig farm, would solemnly forage through the works' dustbins, retrieving all the bits which had been discarded in his absence and returning them to the stores, 'because they might come in handy one day'.

But it wasn't just the 'no hopers', like us, who used to enjoy themselves between races. I remember the 1964 Austrian Grand Prix at Zeltweg which was the first time the Austrians had staged a World Championship round. The circuit was the old airfield number – characterless and desperately bumpy – and the whole meeting was a bit of a disaster. Phil Hill wrote his Cooper off in practice, then did it again in the race, driving the spare car, only this time the thing caught fire and Phil was lucky to escape unscathed. All the top drivers – Graham Hill, Jim Clark, John Surtees and Dan Gurney – dropped out and the eventual winner was Lorenzo Bandini. It was his first, and only, Championship victory. I finished second-to-last, miles behind the leaders, and all the cars finished the race with suspensions falling to bits and rivets working loose.

To take our minds off all this there was a huge post-race party. Jim Clark and Innes Ireland arrived wearing kilts – which wasn't too surprising for a pair of Scots – but Innes being Innes had elected to wear nothing underneath. As the evening progressed Innes became more and more enthusiastic and eventually decided to dance on the table. All the girls became very excited, but it was just too much for Graham Hill who dashed outside and returned with a nice prickly cactus. Poor old Innes and his girlfriend spent the next week occupied with a pair of tweezers and a magnifying glass, pulling out the spines!

On another occasion, we were all sunning ourselves on the beach at Cap Ferrat when the female members of the party decided to go off on pedaloes. Half an hour later they returned, giggling with laughter, with stories of a 'flasher' on the distant rocks. Being a chivalrous bunch, Graham, Bruce McLaren, Chris and I leapt onto the pedaloes and set off to defend the ladies' honour. Unfortunately, by the time we reached the rocks the wicked fellow had disappeared. Undaunted, Graham dived into the water, swam to the headland and promptly dropped his trunks 'to ensure that the girls hadn't made the trip for nothing!'

In those days not all of us could afford to stay in expensive hotels on trips abroad, but we certainly made up for that. We used to go down to Monaco as soon as we could after the previous race and stay for as long as we could after the Grand Prix had taken place, lying in the sun, swimming, haring round the local go-kart track during the day and exploring the hostelries at night. On one occasion we even managed to take over one of the local night clubs, much to the owner's dismay, and were royally entertained by Bruce Abernathy 'in cabaret', until he fell off the stage and broke his ankle!

Chris, Revvie and I were more broke than most - we never actually won a fortune in prize money, let alone got paid for driving - but we discovered a very reasonable little hotel in Cap Ferrat which cost ten francs a night - including dinner! The railway ran past the bottom of the back yard and we were kept awake all night by the trains. In the mornings we would breakfast on the 'terrace', getting showered with soot every time a locomotive steamed past. We called the place the 'Jardin Exotique'.

I really think we used to *enjoy* the racing more in those days too. I realise that today's cars are probably harder to drive physically and, of course, they are more powerful. I remember Denny Hulme making that point at the French Grand Prix in 1974 when he drove the 1966 Brabham Repco in the anniversary parade before stepping back into his McLaren for the race. 'I'd forgotten how much easier they were to drive,' said Denny. 'You really could chuck those cars about. It isn't half as easy to get out of trouble today as it was.'

I'm sure Denny was right. But, on the other hand, races today are much shorter than they were. The 1964 Monaco Grand Prix, for instance, was one hundred laps and took three hours to complete. I was absolutely shattered at the end of it - a mental and physical wreck - and it took me three full days to recover. It was also the first time that I scored Championship points. I finished sixth and, as I stopped in the pits, dazed and exhausted but, I thought, justifiably proud of my one point, Tim Parnell's genial face loomed over the cockpit. 'Eeh lad,' came the bluff Derbyshire tones, 'I thought you would have done better than that.'

In the sixties, too, there was a definite 'off' season, three or four months in which the lads would trek off to Australia, New Zealand and, perhaps, South Africa for the winter racing. Basically, the season consisted of an endless round of parties - the racing was purely incidental, more of an excuse to be there I suppose! These were the days when Grand Prix drivers were prepared to race anything - in this case Tasman Formula cars or sports cars. Of course, it was nothing like Formula One, but we were still racing - after a fashion!

I used to go down to South Africa with friends like David Hobbs, Dickie Attwood, Richard Piper and Paul Hawkins. Paul was an Australian with an outrageous sense of fun, a sports car driver who lived life to the hilt. Paul came from a motor sporting background; his father had been a prominent motorcycle racer, as well as the Victorian high-diving champion. Later in life, apparently, Hawkins Senior was ordained as a Protestant minister, but it was his competitive spirit which his son inherited!

Paul really was a 'True Grit' sort of character, a win or bust merchant. He had more than his fair share of accidents but in between he used to pulverise the opposition in his Ian Walker-owned Lotus 23. He was given his chance in Formula One in 1965, driving a DW Racing Lotus 33, and it was entirely in keeping with his style that he should become only the second man in history to dive into the harbour at Monte Carlo. Fortunately, like Alberto Ascari ten years before, he escaped uninjured, the powerful Australian crawl, learned in the shark-infested waters of the Tasman sea, paid dividends as he struck out towards the Monaco shore. Sadly, Paul was killed in 1968 at Oulton Park, driving a Lola sports car. The car crashed with full tanks and caught fire immediately.

I don't think that the drivers are any more aware of the dangers of the sport than they were in my day or in Stirling's day, but there's such a constant pressure on their time, with the season running virtually all year long and constant testing being the rule, that the tension hardly ever relaxes. Actually, modern drivers don't seem to have the same urge to enjoy themselves together that we did. Pressure from the sponsors is another factor, the need to preserve the image is all-important. Drivers 'on parade' at cocktail parties are expected to be on even better behaviour than normal, whereas I always thought that cocktail parties were for enjoying myself!

I really noticed the change in attitude when I returned to Grand Prix racing in 1971. I had had a good run in Formula 5000 driving for John Surtees, finishing runner-up in the 1971 Championship to Frank Gardner, and it seemed a logical progression to move into Formula One. Top-level racing of any sort is obviously going to be very demanding, to be treated with that much more respect, and so it was hardly surprising that I found Formula 5000 so much more easy-going than Grand Prix racing. In the first two years of the formula (1969 and 1970) I drove Lolas for Jackie Epstein, starting with the original T142 then moving on to the T190 and finally the T192. I finished third in the Championship in both years but signed on with 'Big John' Surtees for 1971.

I think people thought it was a pretty unholy alliance at first glance because our temperaments were poles apart. I don't think he understood a thing I said and I certainly didn't understand a thing he said - so we muddled along fine! Old John always had the reputation of being a rather austere individual but I think his bark was worse than his bite and, after I had been there a year or so, he seemed to change, to mellow towards my way of thinking. He knew well enough what I was like and he was sufficiently shrewd to realise that he did not stand a chance of influencing my life-style. In the end, in fact, I think I influenced his. He started to have a good time himself, which was good to see. Secretly, John enjoys a good party as much as any of us, even if he did adopt the role of the schoolmaster who must always set a good example to his pupils.

I must say I did enjoy those years in Formula 5000. There were a lot of 'characters' in the game, but they were men who were destined never to become serious Formula One contenders. There were some who had tried Formula One and failed and a few who later moved up to Formula One only to slip back again. I think I must have been unique, having been in Formula One four or five years earlier, quitting the sport for bikes, returning in Formula 5000 and then going back to Formula One again!

Those early Formula 5000 drivers really were quite outrageous characters. Tony Lanfranchi, Jackie Epstein, Peter Gethin, Gordon Spice, Dave Prophet, Ulf Norinder, who used to throw week-long parties up at his place in Sweden - we all got on very well together. I suppose we did tend to write off too many cars out of sheer enthusiasm, which didn't go down well with the owners, but the racing got better and better, particularly in my last season, 1971.

It certainly gave me another chance in Formula One when John promoted me to the Grand Prix team at Monza in 1971. It was a race I thoroughly enjoyed with a terrific photo-finish which Peter Gethin won by a whisker. I finished fourth after actually having led the race on a couple of occasions – a situation which staggered quite a few people and delighted 'Big John'! So there I was, back in Formula One full-time for 1972.

The atmosphere was very alien to me; the vast majority of my fellow drivers were a stern lot and quite withdrawn. Friends like Chris Amon and Peter Revson were taking the whole business much more seriously than in the old days and Graham Hill was deeply involved with his own team. The only driver whose attitude seemed to coincide with mine was James Hunt who always seemed like a man out to do his own thing. But I never really knew James that well. Another character around in those days whom I later got to know and like very much was Denny Hulme. Denny is not the easiest of people to get to know – he doesn't suffer fools gladly – but he's a very forthright bloke with a wicked sense of humour. We really became good friends out in New Zealand when we had both retired, doing a couple of Economy Runs together and having a hilarious time. Neither of us had a clue how to work out the fuel consumption figures and we had to ask the accompanying scrutineers to do it. They just shook their heads in disbelief. I also 'converted' Denny to bikes and now he loves roaring off into the lava hills behind his home.

But things were so different when we were racing. Drivers would disappear into the motor homes immediately after practice and then be whisked away to their hotels. Mechanics would be working through the night sorting out endless modifications and team managers were locked in their 'decompression chambers' getting their ears bashed. It was actually a very lonely business. After practice I used to get back to the hotel, sit and read a book, have my dinner and go to bed.

One person who did help to keep me sane, however, was Rob Walker. In fact, Rob seemed to follow me around, first with Surtees, then with the 'Yardley Mac'. He is the most down-to-earth and sane man I have ever met, and a true gentleman who has been in motor racing since 1934 and had drivers of the calibre of Moss, Collins, Salvadori, Parnell, Brooks, Brabham, Trintignant, Hill, Ireland, Bonnier and Siffert on his books. He has a fund of amusing stories guaranteed to cheer anyone up after the worst possible practice session and he obviously understood the frustrations I was feeling. It was Rob who used to insist that I had a couple of glasses of wine with dinner the night before a race. I think he believed that I would suffer from withdrawal symptoms if I didn't! And his lovely wife Bette used to bake tins full of my favourite parkin as a reward for turning in good practice times.

I wouldn't want people to think that I was miserable all the time. I did enjoy the racing; it was great to be able to have a real go at Stewart in Kyalami in 1972, and who knows what might have happened if that rear suspension bolt hadn't sheared off. I thoroughly enjoyed leading the International Trophy Race at Silverstone that same year before those mechanical gremlins forced the Surtees' pressure cap off, and I was really pleased with my drive at Monza when I finished second to Fittipaldi – my best ever Grand Prix result – in spite of the fact that my airbox flew off on lap 19!

I think I was most frustrated by the limitations imposed by my inability to set up the car. I basically lacked the mechanical background of someone like John Surtees, and my 'training' in the sixties had left a lot to be desired mechanically. After the disastrous 1973 season with Surtees I was delighted to be offered the Yardley McLaren drive in '74 as I regarded the McLaren as a very good car indeed. My problem with McLaren was that everything was taken that much *more* seriously; it almost got to the stage where I was nervous of being seen speaking to other drivers in case people thought I was giving trade secrets away!

Grand Prix racing had become an incredibly time-consuming business. Drivers were forced into living a kind of bridegroom existence, with motor racing as the wife. I think why James Hunt and the Hesketh team were criticised so much is because they were obviously out to enjoy themselves *off* the track. What a lot of people didn't seem to realise was that they did take their racing very seriously indeed – in fact, anyone who doesn't has to be an idiot. Drivers understand the nature of the sport and nobody is going to put himself or his fellow drivers unnecessarily at risk by going out on the track under the influence of alcohol.

I know there were some people who thought that I always used to drink before I raced. I'm not *that* crazy! I enjoy life too much to try to throw it away. To be honest, there were two occasions in my career when I *did* compete 'under the influence', but certainly never when I was in Formula One.

The first time was on my twenty-first birthday when I was racing at a bike meeting at Snetterton and all the lads brought along bottles of champagne. I managed to knock quite a lot of this back in between practice and the race itself and I remember wheeling my Norton to the startline in a fairly 'merry' mood. Nothing untoward happened but I didn't make that mistake again until much later. On the second occasion I was sharing a 2-litre Lola with another driver at one of the Nurburgring 1000km races in the early seventies. We were both out until five o'clock on race-day morning and were both feeling very much the worse for wear when the race started. We tossed up to see who should stick his head in the lion's mouth and drive first and, as I was more accustomed to drinking the night away than he was, it was maybe just as well that I lost! Fortunately a wheel fell off fairly early on and I was able to abandon the car without any drama.

Personally, I think that it's a great shame that Grand Prix racing has got to its current, somewhat boring state. I appreciate that it's a much more professional business today, considerably more so than when I last raced, and I realise that the extra pressures of big money sponsorship have to be accepted as part of the game. The financial rewards are enormous now, but the penalty is being paid by the drivers in terms of sheer enjoyment. Frankly, I find that very sad.

2 Finance and early days behind the wheel

STIRLING MOSS

The financial content of Grand Prix racing has improved out of all recognition since my day. Perhaps, though, it has got out of hand.

Any discussion of drivers' incomes puts me in an ambiguous situation. When I was racing in the fifties and sixties, I was all for earning as much as I could get. Often, later in my career, I would hold out for a greater sum than the organisers might originally have offered - and usually I got it. Remember, though, that as far as the relationship between driver and organiser was concerned, the boot was firmly on the other foot compared with today. The theory was that a race would take place whatever the situation, and that a crowd would arrive to watch it. Drivers of note were confidently expected because it was only by racing consistently that such men could earn their living. Organisers might have paid a bit more starting money for the World Champion (or in my case, more often than not, the runner-up!), but there was never any question of any competitor being able to hold an organiser up for ransom. It was no good me pouting my lower lip and saying, 'Look here, I'm Stirling Moss, so you will pay me such and such a figure'. If I had they would just as likely have said, 'OK, *you* may not be coming, but we've still got Hawthorn, Collins, Behra, Musso and Bonnier, any of whom will attract a good crowd'.

Nor, of course, could a driver rely on sponsorship for a massive income as financial support from major companies was simply not forthcoming when I was racing. You were lucky, in the early days, to benefit from as much as a free gallon of oil, which, in fact, was exactly what I did get in my first year of single-seater racing. It was a five-gallon drum of an oil called Sternol, a deal negotiated with my father. All right, perhaps there's many a Formula Ford driver today who would be almost as happy as I was with such a gesture, but the point is that despite winning a whole bunch of races the prospect of another five-gallon drum was no more forthcoming than that of a free engine. Occasionally I used to receive the odd trade bonus and so on, but it wasn't until I joined up with Leslie Johnson in the very early fifties, driving sports Jaguars, that I actually earned any real money for racing.

Leslie went, on my behalf, to Shell-Mex, who offered me my first ever big contract - £1,000 for one year. Later, I changed over to BP and this association continued for many years. I actually had a contract with Ferodo to use their brake linings, which ran from 1949, but the amount was very little indeed. Oddly enough, this deal still runs; it's probably the longest-running racing contract ever!

Right up until not long before my retirement I was still *buying* my racing tyres from Dunlop; they gave me a discount of 50 per cent then finally 66 per cent. Only at the very end of my career did I get my tyres free of charge - the final two years, in fact! That was the way it was in those days - you simply couldn't take anything for granted. If you wanted some new demon tweak, or a special set of tyres, or a set of springs, you had to go out and buy it - if someone else hadn't got there first.

Obviously, as a professional full-time driver, I was keen on making money. But I regarded the money I earned not as something to invest, or with which to buy huge houses in Monte Carlo, but as a means by which I could continue racing. As a man who was reckoning on earning all his money from motor racing, I was more than delighted when someone offered me a drive, because I could see that the more I raced, the more I would earn. When I joined Aston Martin to lead the team in the mid-fifties I was given a contract worth £50. Similarly when I drove for the Rootes Group in the Alpine Rally, which took two weeks including practice, again I received fifty quid. Expenses were paid, but there were few perks. However, £50 in those days was still good money as far as I was concerned.

Of course, as time went on my income increased. When I raced for Mercedes-Benz in 1955 I received 20 dollars a day expenses on which to live, plus a contract worth, I think, £1,000, which was enormous. On top of that we were allowed to keep 90 per cent of our winnings - a considerable amount that year. Normally one worked on a 50-50 basis but Mercedes could afford to be generous - or maybe they regarded it as an extra incentive.

With Rob Walker, for whom I raced from 1958 to 1962, I had no contract fee, in fact no contract at all, but I did get 60 per cent of the starting and prize money. My arrangement there was that if Rob chose to run Maurice Trintignant instead of myself (when I might be driving for someone else, for instance, as occasionally happened) Rob would take the normal 50 per cent of the money. With me, the 40 per cent he would get was likely to be about the same in terms of real money simply through my being able to command a greater starting fee than Maurice. That may sound tough, I'm not sure, but I was trying to be fair both to myself and to Rob, who of course was a private owner without factory support. The relationship between Rob and myself was a very special one. I respected him and he respected me, and we both knew that neither would let the other down. It was because of that understanding that I never had any kind of contract with Rob, there just wasn't the need. As far as I was concerned he did as much for British motor racing as anybody and while he was going racing, so was I.

Although he was a private entrant, Rob of course did possess a few bob and I don't think, in those days anyway, that running a racing team took too much of his capital. Later, as racing became vastly more expensive, people like him were forced out. But even earlier than that there were plenty of British owners, entrants and builders who found it an expensive business to campaign around Europe in search of international success and prestige.

As early as 1950 I found myself racing for John Heath and his bravely intended but under-financed HWM Formula Two team. Heath's ambition was to beat the Ferraris, Maseratis and so on at their own game, just as it was Tony Vandervell's a few years later. But rather like me, Heath looked forward to winning money with the aim not of suddenly becoming rich but so as to afford to go on to the next race. When I first drove for John, my contract paid me 25 per cent of the starting money; the remaining 75 per cent went on running the car, paying the mechanics, covering depreciation on the vehicles and so on. Normally the starting money was around £150-200 an event, so with one race every two weeks I was actually earning £50 a fortnight. Well, £50 then was a lot more than it is now but even so I could hardly afford to stay at the Ritz. This was a time when I was travelling around Europe at my own expense, and there's no doubt that we were forced to live fairly frugally. At my age (about 20), I hardly expected to live a life of luxury; on the other hand HWM were, as far as this country was concerned, a major team. They were competing with the might of overseas manufacturers, usually on foreign soil. The races I drove in included a multitude of 'Grands Prix' - not World Championship events perhaps but relatively big-time nevertheless.

At no time did I feel hard done by. John Heath had, as far as I was concerned, given me a big break. I had every reason to be thankful. The fact that I could not live very grandly, that I had to choose my food rather carefully (one course and no coffee for dinner, snacks on the road during the day!) came as no real hardship; this was the way it had to be if one wanted to go on racing abroad.

Not that I was unaware of the value of being something of a celebrity - perhaps I should say a curiosity - and even when I first started I had some box-office value through being so young. Here was a twenty-year-old Englishman driving an English car, not a common combination in 1950, especially in France and Italy. We had no hope of winning, but through being young and presenting a fresh challenge to the locals I suppose I did do better than some of the others as far as starting money was concerned. A bit later, when I had established a certain reputation for having a good go, I used to wave to the crowd on the warm-up lap and the cooling-down lap. This encouraged them to wave back and so the organisers quickly decided that I must be a frightfully popular chap! Anyway, it was enough to persuade them into offering me more money to return next year.

The 'starting money' idea is a good one. It signifies that the organiser is prepared to pay you according to your value to him. If you aren't going to bring a crowd through the gates, then why should he want you? On the other hand if you *are* a bit of a draw, then he'll pay you well. It was the kind of deal which I always thought was very fair. If a driver who wasn't getting paid much wanted to do something about it, then it was up to him to beat you. That way he not only earned the prize money, but was immediately worth more starting money next time.

Today's way of doing things, with Bernie Ecclestone negotiating with the organisers and then handing out the money on a special - and secret - sliding-scale according to whether or not you are a full member of FOCA (Formula One Constructors Association) is rather different. Bernie's way still rewards effort, because the faster you go in practice the more money you, or rather your team, will receive, but it does make it difficult for a driver to judge his real worth as a crowd-puller.

For instance, if Alan Jones makes a bad start, drives through the field to lead the race and then busts the engine, the Williams team will receive less than the winner, who, for the purpose of our example, is Jody Scheckter. That's reasonable enough, but at the next race it's Jones the crowd will want to see, rather than Jody. However, the deal with the next lot of organisers has already been done - they merely pay one lump sum for which a full grid of F1 cars is guaranteed. Jones is left pondering how to play it. If he continues to please the crowd with his great deeds of derring-do, he will only earn more money for Frank Williams if he actually finishes. Better, perhaps, to back off and settle for a safe second place, or third, rather than go for broke and victory. I'm sure that Jones does not, in fact, lie awake at nights worrying about such matters, because he is the sort of genuine racer who would go for broke under any circumstances. But there are those drivers who might 'cruise' to protect their World Championship position on the one hand without forfeiting their income on the other.

For the smaller teams, particularly, the pressure just to *finish* a Grand Prix is enormous. To be guaranteed a place amid next year's Grand Prix 'circus,' World Championship points are a must. Fair enough, but the system must tempt the team manager of such an outfit, seeing his car fight its way into sixth place, to hang out a signal saying 'Hold'. The driver may want to try for fifth or fourth, perhaps spinning off in the process, perhaps not, but the rules of the game – Bernie's rules, not those of FISA (Fédération Internationale Sportive Automobile) – sometimes make such a move unwise.

There is no doubt, mark you, that the financing of the sport has *had* to change since my day. Things have got far too expensive to gamble on doing well next race in order to pay for the disasters of the last. Big-figure sponsorship is an absolute necessity as are proper, long-term agreements of the type engineered by Bernie. Teams must be able to plan the whole season through, secure in the knowledge that funds from organisers will be consistently available in approximately the right quantities. But to run a racing car today is, I think, unreasonably expensive, even though the sophistication and the precision of the machine are fantastic compared with twenty or thirty years ago. I look at the way a Brabham or a Lotus is built and then try to think of the way John Heath put together his HWMs. The task is impossible, because there is no comparison. Heath used to weld a couple of large tubes together, thus creating the frame, and then go round road car manufacturers buying standard parts which he would somehow attach to his chassis. I think the only parts specially built for a *racing* car were the Arfin brakes and Borani wheels. All the others would be modified production car components. The car was literally a Bitza – you know, bitza this and bitza that. This hardly made for reliability, or indeed safety, but it was a cheap way of doing things, and for Heath the only way.

Drivers of the eighties find themselves piloting racing projectiles, constructed virtually to aerospace standards, with all the accompanying costs. The complexity of the business has escalated perhaps to a point of no return and one wonders just how much more sophisticated and expensive things can become. Certainly it has gone way, way beyond the idea of living on a week to week basis and hoping blindly that your man wins next time out.

In the fifties, the way to earn money, either as a team or as a driver, was to race as often as possible. I certainly raced very frequently indeed and as a result I believe I was the highest paid racing driver in road racing. There may have been a few drivers in America, racing in USAC (Indianapolis style) or NASCAR (saloon cars on oval tracks) events, who earned more than me, but as a road racer I always figured, from 1954 onwards, that I enjoyed the highest income. Fangio, I'm sure, earned a lot more than I did at Mercedes, but against that I raced in a lot more events than he did – I had to. When I went to Silverstone to take part in, say, the International Trophy, or to Goodwood for the Glover Trophy, I might get three or four hundred pounds, but the organisers would expect me to drive four or five cars. I would take part in the sports car race, the touring car race, the GT race and the Formula One race – and if there was an F2 race on the programme, I'd run in that as well! If I'd have said, 'Look, I'm only prepared to do the F1 race,' I suppose I might still have been paid the £400, I'm not sure. I did know that by competing in all the events open to me I was giving my money's worth, and enjoying myself as well.

In retrospect, it amazes me how often one put one's reputation and one's neck on the line without being paid. In the early fifties there was a thing called the 'Race of the Champions' which was a sports car race, all of us in XK120 Jaguars, and nothing to do with the modern F1 race of the same name. The idea was that the champions from various categories of racing pitched in against each other in identical machinery. It wasn't an enormously important affair, but it was of considerable interest to the public and, of course, very useful publicity for Jaguar. There you were, prepared to race against all these other champions to see if you were as good, with virtually everything to lose and little to gain. Certainly nothing to gain financially because the idea of paying us never crossed anyone's mind!

I did expect to get paid if I drove for an established team, of course. This was the way in which I supplemented my income from Grand Prix racing. By today's standards, the money I was getting was laughably small and clearly the drivers of the eighties work out the financial aspect of things much more effectively than I did. But then again I was not like them; I enjoyed all kinds of racing to the extent that I would have a go for no money at all rather than lose the drive through trying to be too greedy.

I am bound to say that I do not believe contemporary racing drivers really deserve the huge amounts they earn. But then, I don't believe that film stars deserve what they get either. Of course, racing is an extremely hazardous business, and the dangers are obvious. But it's no good saying, 'I'm risking my neck, so I must be worth a million pounds a year'. I don't think you can put any sort of monetary value on a person's life. I'm inclined to feel that anyone who loves motor racing takes part not just to get rich quick. Pleasure, excitement, exhilaration, call it what you will, is a major attraction too. If one accepts these days that drivers do *not* get any pleasure out of racing then one has to say that yes, they *are* earning the money – it's the only thing left. I think it's a terrible shame that this may be so and I would like to see the money drop down and the enjoyment come up.

Personally I feel that for anybody, whether a racing driver, an actor, a politician or a businessman, to earn much more than a quarter of a million pounds a year is almost immoral. Certainly, in motor racing there can be very little incentive to earn an extra couple of thousand in prize money or bonuses when you've already got three hundred thousand – or perhaps three million – in the bank. I appreciate that a lot of drivers in Grand Prix racing do not get anything like a quarter of a million. Some have to find their own sponsors, to buy their way into a drive. This was the case in 1979 with both of the works Shadow drivers, for instance. Too often, it seems that certain people are offered top drives not because of their ability but because of the money and influence they can bring to bear. The paradox is that while Grand Prix racing is a 'closed shop', with everyone having to qualify for the required Super Licence, a new guy always seems to be able to worm his way in if he waves his cheque book enough times. There is nothing wrong in paying your way in motor racing; in my day there were plenty doing just that and we called them private owners. The difference now is that genuine privateers have been hounded out and it is the factory teams to which newcomers are forced to turn. Again, that in itself is all right just so long as the rich kid is not occupying a seat which would be better served by other more talented but less wealthy drivers. When Mercedes turned me down early in 1954 they did so because they felt, quite rightly, that I had not proved my true worth. I'm sure that if my then manager, Ken

Gregory, had offered them a million pounds (which we did not have, nor even a fraction of the amount) their answer would have been the same. Today, I fear that most teams would tend to grab the money and worry about the man's ability later.

As a business, motor racing has failed. It has priced itself out of the market, except for those with major funds at their disposal. If I were twenty-five years old today and attempting to break into Grand Prix racing I doubt if I would succeed. I managed it in 1954 because my family and I could just about scrape together enough money to buy a reasonably competitive car. In fact, we paid five million lire for the 250F Maserati, which worked out at £3,400. That was a lot of cash but the car was brand new and Maserati were prepared to make available the latest works mods whenever they had been perfected. I still had to pay for them, however!

Even in those days running a car cost more than buying it and so the full season might have cost us a total of £10,000. It did not end up being that pricey because towards the end Maserati themselves stepped in and asked me to lead their official team. The point is that the figure of £10,000 in 1954 for buying and maintaining a new, sophisticated Grand Prix car, has to be compared with what is necessary today. Obviously it is impossible to be exact, but I am told that Bernie Ecclestone was demanding half a million pounds from Rupert Keegan to include him in the Brabham 'B' team for 1980 – and probably Bernie's profit would not have been excessive even at this figure. That's fifty times more than it was costing me, many times more in real terms even allowing for raging inflation.

The cost of Grand Prix racing, like the sums the top drivers earn, is out of proportion to what the sport actually represents. It has gone over the top both technically and commercially. I wish I had made more out of my success, that's only natural, but in terms of sheer enjoyment I reckon I was richer at the time than any of today's superstars. My best year, not surprisingly, came with my last full season, 1961. My total gross income was £32,700 out of which I had to pay my manager, my secretary, travel bills, hotels, food and everything else. I seem to remember I paid tax on about £8,000, the rest went on overheads and expenses. Eight thousand then was very good money. It would be about eighty thousand today, I suppose. On the other hand, the likes of James Hunt, Niki Lauda, Jody Scheckter and perhaps Alan Jones have allegedly been earning a million a year – quite a difference.

The most money I made out of one race was the thousand pounds paid by the organisers of the European Grand Prix at the Nurburgring in 1961. I split that with Rob Walker, but for winning he would have paid me a bonus which might have been another thousand pounds. Incidentally, I would normally give the mechanics 10 per cent of my prize money before splitting the remainder with Rob. I wonder if that happens today . . . .

I hardly need to emphasise that the major reason why drivers can make so much more today is the upsurge of commercial involvement. The guys of the eighties are clearly much smarter than I was, and I must admit I was used rather a lot with no reimbursement. People would ask you to come to a garage opening, to perform the ceremony of cutting the tape or whatever, and you did. Or rather, I did. I never dreamt of submitting an account because, perhaps naively, I was happy to go along as a genuine favour, hoping I would maybe get a decent meal. Nowadays I certainly do present a bill – a fairly large one!

Endorsements used to bring in a small amount as one usually got a percentage of what was sold. Steering wheels and driving gloves were the sort of things I helped to advertise – not exactly breaking into the big-time. If I made a few hundred here and there I reckoned I was doing well.

It may be that my manager should have done better on my behalf – he was there to organise the financial side after all! Looking at it seriously, though, I reckon that Ken did pretty well. Today Ken is an extraordinarily successful businessman and I'm satisfied he did the best job he could for me. I'm sure that if he could have made his money working with S. Moss, then he would have done. Sadly the opportunities just were not there in my day. If Ken had gone along to, let's say, Fabergé, and said, 'Look, I've got this guy who can win anything and who's prepared to appear in your ads on television and so on, and we want £10,000,' they would have laughed in his face. Maybe they would have come up with £500 and a bottle of perfume, probably not even that, because that kind of personality marketing was barely known in the fifties, outside of Denis Compton and Brylcream ... and there wasn't much hope for me there! In any case really big sums simply were not paid, not in Europe anyway. I appeared in a few advertisements, but my fees hardly busted anyone's budget. I did a series of ads for BP and in the end we negotiated a deal whereby I received free petrol for my private motoring. I also did an ad for a cigarette firm and I think I received a hundred pounds for that, and a few free smokes.

In 1961 Ferrari offered me a contract worth £10,000. It was the biggest deal, money-wise, that had been put together up to that time. I will talk about my relationship with Ferrari in a later chapter, but unfortunately for me any big money I hoped to make over subsequent seasons was lost once I had crashed. My predicament at that point was even more serious than it would be for one of today's top drivers. The Goodwood accident put me out of racing and left me with no immediate way of earning an income. I was thirty-three years old with no other strings to my bow, no big investments and no business interests to fall back on. Oddly, it was only *after* I had retired that I began to realise just how much, as a driver, I might have been able to make. I assumed to start with that my name would remain sufficiently well-known for a year or so to provide me with some kind of living. I hoped to be able to make some money, therefore, out of being a *recently* retired racing driver, but what staggered me was that the situation never changed. Even now, eighteen years after my crash, I am still earning my living from being retired, if one can say such a thing. Indeed today I am earning a very much larger amount from personal appearances and the like than I did when I was racing. Of course, that sort of thing is now the vogue and I am only lucky that I did enough when I was actually competing to keep my name alive so long afterwards. I work at it, mark you, but surprisingly the fact that I am now racing again, a bit in historics and rather more in saloon cars, has made no difference at all. Very few people, outside of dedicated enthusiasts, realise that I do occasionally get back into a racing car. My 'return to the tracks' has hardly affected my income at all. What it has done is given me a great deal of pleasure at a time in my life when theoretically, perhaps, I should be past it!

I have always been addicted to motor racing, and so have thousands of others. I'm sure that every driver starts off the same way: he wants desperately to have a go, to reach Formula One standard, to win a Grand Prix, to become World Champion. There is the addiction of being able to drive faster than the other guy, of getting past him and saying, 'Come on, boy, now you try and catch me'. There is the addiction of controlling a high-powered racing car, of going into a corner and adjusting the wheel, feeling the power-breaking traction at the rear wheels, of contending with the natural hazards of road racing. Today, I believe that the initial addiction, the early striving for success, turns into an addiction to money. Then, when it gets to the point where you've made your first two million – points reached by James Hunt and Niki Lauda – even the money becomes unimportant.

It seems to be a vicious spiral from which, for many drivers, there can be no escape except to abandon the sport for some other interest.

MIKE HAILWOOD

I signed my first 'big money' contract when I was riding bikes for the Italian MV factory in the early sixties. It was worth the princely sum of two million lire (about twelve hundred pounds in those days) and a lot of money for a biker. By the time I left MV at the end of '65 I think they had worked it up to about twelve million lire (something over seven thousand pounds), a veritable fortune!

At the same time, when I joined Reg Parnell's Formula One team in 1963, I paid him five thousand pounds, which was an awful lot of money. Yes, paid-for drives existed, even in those days, and there was Hailwood digging deep into his piggy-bank to try to break into the then highly sophisticated world of Grand Prix racing. I suppose I arrived at the start of the rent-a-drive trend. Revvie (Peter Revson) was paying for his drives too, and we were under the strictest instructions not to do anything silly in practice, simply because if anything broke we had no spare parts for the cars. And if we didn't start the race, of course, the team didn't collect any start money!

Reg Parnell had lost his sponsors at the end of 1962 so this happy band of privateers provided a way of meeting expenses. Sadly, Reg died during the winter of '63 and his son Tim took over. Tim is a great big, lovable, cuddly guy who used to do a bit of driving himself until his bulk assumed proportions too great to be squeezed into even the widest cockpit! I remember one race in that year when the Parnell team actually ran six cars: Tim in a Lotus V8, Chris Amon and myself in Lola Mark 4s, Ron Carter, Philip Robinson and André Pilette in 4-cylinder Lotuses, which were hopelessly outclassed.

In spite of my dismal results on the race track, in retrospect I think I got quite a good deal. Up until the sixties Formula One drivers were either contracted to factory teams or they were private owners racing their own cars, or possibly racing on behalf of a benefactor. The waving of cheque books to buy into a drive was not common practice. Very few competitors earned much money compared to today's standards, not even Graham Hill or Jimmy Clark at that stage, but the general idea was that you either had enough talent to earn a team drive or you had enough money to finance yourself completely. I had neither! Today my £5,000 wouldn't even buy half an engine. But as it was, with the Parnell team I did twenty-four races during the period 1963-65 and at the end I had my £5,000 returned!

I also got the opportunity to race on the same track as Graham Hill and Jimmy Clark (I wouldn't say I got the chance to race *against* them, they were nearly always three or four laps ahead of me!). Clark was the greatest racing driver I ever saw. He was a rather nervous type, particularly before a race, but he was good fun. Later, when I returned to racing in the seventies, I was competing against Jackie Stewart at his peak. As I was driving rather more competitive cars I was able to give a better account of myself against Jackie. But I think that Stewart was without a doubt the most complete racing driver. In fact, he was so good both on and off the track that it was a little frightening.

I certainly didn't earn any real money out of car racing until I returned to Formula One in the seventies, and for a long time my income from bike racing used to subsidise my car racing. Then, when I finally abandoned bikes again to concentrate on cars, I managed to do well enough to make a living on four wheels instead of two. But money was never the be-all and end-all. It was very nice to win a race and see the pound notes coming in, but it was always the achievement rather than the reward that mattered most to me.

However, driving for 'Big John' in the seventies wasn't the most lucrative thing in the world, particularly in '73 when I didn't score any Championship points at all! But I did get a lot of satisfaction from winning the European Formula Two Championship in the Surtees TS10 in 1972. The atmosphere in Formula Two was much better than in Formula One for me – not so tense and dominated by business interests.

When I joined McLaren for the 1974 season I passed the five-figure mark for the first time; for that year I signed a contract with Yardley worth £10,000. It was the most I ever earned out of Formula One. I had had several other offers which weren't so attractive. I would have joined the Marlboro McLaren set-up – if they had asked me! – or Ferrari. I knew old Enzo Ferrari quite well, I used to have lunch with him quite often in my bike racing days and I got on well with him. Unfortunately, *they* never asked me!

But seriously, I thought that the McLaren M23 was the best car around at the time and, although I could have got more money elsewhere, I was prepared to settle for less in order to be able to drive one. My assessment proved correct too when Emerson won the 1974 Championship in the McLaren. And I have reason to be thankful that I was driving one at the Nurburgring when I crashed. I'm convinced that my injuries would have been much more serious than they were had I been driving anything else.

Had I not been forced to retire after my accident I'm not sure what I would have done. Yardley pulled out of motor racing at the end of the season and there was no room for me in the Marlboro McLaren team. I think I might have joined Graham Hill who was setting up his new team. I knew and liked Graham tremendously. We had known each other a long time and, I suppose, we understood each other's temperaments. But it was not to be.

I can't honestly say that I thought we were underpaid in those days, but I *do* think that *some* drivers are overpaid today.

Of course, motor racing is a very dangerous sport, mistakes are punished very harshly, and those taking part should be paid accordingly. It is much more professional, much more of a business today than it was in the old days and it would obviously be as unwise as it is impossible to take part in Formula One 'just for the hell of it'. But to me contract fees of a million pounds or more do seem ridiculously excessive. Let me explain.

Surely paying a bloke a million pounds before he has even sat in a car must be counter-productive? If a driver can earn a million out of endorsements or prize money, or by racing in eight different categories, then good luck to him. That's fine. But if a guy already has that much in the bank before he even starts, where's the incentive to go out and actually earn it? I know that if I had that much money stashed away I'd try to make sure I lived until the end of the year so that I could enjoy myself spending it!

If that meant going slower or not trying as hard as I should, then that's the way it would be. It's only human nature. On the other hand, if I hadn't got a million in my pocket and the only way I could see myself getting it was to put my foot down a bit harder or a bit earlier, then I imagine I would do that too. There is a danger that by dishing out vast sums to some drivers before the season even starts then they may not give of their best. Of course, drivers aren't concentrating on their earning power while they are engaged in the heat of battle! They have too many other things to occupy their minds. But subconsciously it could affect their performance.

Pay a driver a million before he starts the year and then say to him, 'Every time you pass the man in front I will give you another £1,000', and the chances are he won't put himself out all that much. Pay him half a million and say, 'The other £500,000 must be earned from results', and he will try pretty hard. Don't pay him anything and tell him, 'A hundred thousand is yours every time you win', and he'll be flat out ninety per cent of the time. I realise that the last course is unrealistic but I think it illustrates my point. I'm not against big money coming into the sport, I'm just concerned about the way it is being spent.

I am obviously not talking about *all* drivers, only the select handful of top rankers who can virtually name their price with no strings attached. The newcomers to Formula One are just as keen, just as hungry and just as anxious to prove themselves as newcomers to any sport. A number of them, like myself in the mid-sixties, have had to pay the constructors for their drives. Elio de Angelis, for example, is paying Colin Chapman to drive the Essex Lotus, and he's turned in some pretty impressive performances. Nobody goes racing in the first place just for the money!

I know I was attracted to bike racing, and subsequently to cars, in the first place because they interested me, and in the second place, because they were the only things I could take seriously for more than five minutes at a time! I'm sure all the 'new boys' are just as enthusiastic as we were – in fact, they've probably got to be *more* determined to succeed today because the competition is ferocious and the sport so prohibitively expensive. The problems occur when they are well-established and the money element seems to become more and more important. Anyone in any profession who is rewarded a year in advance – and handsomely – must tend towards a certain smugness, which eventually blunts the sharp edge of ambition.

I must admit motor racing today does seem to be surrounded by an extra aura of glamour, one which I wasn't aware of when I was taking part. The huge driver fees, the demands of the Constructors' Association, the vast overheads of running a Grand Prix, the cost of every engine and every tyre, the commercial viability of the sport from the sponsors' viewpoint – it all has to come from somewhere, and that somewhere is still the motor sport fan, the man-in-the-street. Motor racing depends on its public. They may not have to attend a Grand Prix to see it because television covers the world, but the public *must* maintain its interest in order that the TV companies continue their coverage. I wonder though how much longer spectators will put up with third-rate amenities, coupled with a rate of increase in admission charges which makes inflation look positively sluggish?

I know I was never really aware of these problems when I was still racing. I was too involved with the problems on the track to be particularly concerned with what was going on outside. But since I have become a spectator myself, I can appreciate the situation. For decent seats it can cost a family of four way over £100 to watch the British Grand Prix, taking travelling costs, meals, drinks, etc. into account. Yet spectators are still likely to get soaking wet, stuck in the mud, have to queue for hours in traffic jams to get into the circuit, then queue to go to the loo when they get there, and still only get to view the proceedings from a remote vantage point because safety precautions now require the audience to be suitably separated from the ultra-fast Grand Prix cars.

I honestly think that it's about time the sport took a long hard look at its priorities and started to give good value for all that money that is being spent on it.

3 Patriotism and loyalty

STIRLING MOSS

Patriotism is not precisely the same as loyalty, but the idea of not letting the side down is common to both qualities. Immediately, one thinks of the sudden 'retirements' from Grand Prix racing in 1979 of James Hunt and Niki Lauda. Now, to me, there is no question that if a driver decides he has had enough of racing, he should stop as soon as possible, by which I mean at the end of the season. I do not go along with quitting half-way through a year, as Hunt did, and especially not half-way through practice, as Lauda did in Canada.

If drivers were still classified as amateurs, driving cars which belonged to them, or for sheer pleasure, circumstances would obviously be different. But they are, as I've already said, full-time professionals in every sense. They are all under contract and the majority earn large sums of money, either from personal sponsors or direct from their team. Any attempt to get out of racing while they are still obligated, legally and financially, to their employer or sponsor seems at best ill-advised and at worst downright traitorous.

I suppose in the case of Hunt that if he felt *that* nervous about it he should have pulled out – as indeed he did. At least he was polite enough to discuss the matter with his team. What I regard as a bit poor was his lack of discretion; once he thought he was free, as I understand it, he was on the phone to Ligier, who at the time had a much better car than Wolf, to discuss whether they could take him on. In fact, I believe they would have done so had the Wolf people not put their collective foot down and threatened legal action, something they were more than entitled to do.

The original impression I received from Hunt's retirement was that he had lost confidence in himself as well as his team and that he had become disillusioned with Grand Prix racing. By being subsequently linked with Ligier it seemed he had changed his mind at a point when there ought to have been no going back. Could the thought of more money, and a greater chance of success, have become more important to him than basic loyalty? I like to think not, but the doubt remains.

For a variety of reasons, some of my own making, I often raced cars which were too slow or too unreliable to have much of a chance, but boy, I still had a real go, and when I did manage to win it was all the more satisfying. I can see that today the driver has far less opportunity than I did of compensating for lack of basic speed, but to back out as James did and then secretly try to do a deal with someone else is, I feel, not exactly cricket - or motor sport.

My principle of racing always was, 'I would rather lose a race driving fast enough to win it, than win one driving slow enough to lose it'. I chased success because that was my goal, but the end product did not matter as much to me as how I achieved it. Perhaps this is not the correct attitude. Jackie Stewart, maybe, had the right idea in winning at the slowest speed possible. But I still feel that the whole reason for racing is to compete, and to compete means driving as fast as possible, whatever the circumstances.

The manner of Niki Lauda's withdrawal was more disappointing still. He waited until the car was all prepared - it was a brand new one, the first time out for the Cosworth-engined Brabham - and practice already under way. Niki is clearly a complex character, a perfectionist and a difficult man to fully understand - or appreciate. Possibly, he was a much greater driver than any of us really knew. However, the bare facts of the matter are that the thought suddenly hit him, while he was driving round during the first practice session in Montreal, that he should chuck it in there and then. And he did. And I have to say, reluctantly in Niki's case, that I cannot condone such a decision. Again, it looked, on the surface, as if here was a man who had had a bad season and hadn't got the guts or determination to see things out. In fact, nobody can accuse Niki Lauda, one of the supermen of the seventies, of lacking courage. His return after being severely burned was fantastic. I believe there was more behind his sudden retirement than meets the eye and I feel it's just a shame that he could not have worked things out a little better.

Having competed for so many years in the role of the underdog I can fully understand how frustrating it can be to see the opposition running away from you, or find your car constantly failing under you. When I drove for HWM, it was intensely annoying to watch the Ferraris pull right away down the straight, even though I soon learnt the technique of slip streaming. I ought to explain here that in the days when cars of widely differing power outputs raced against each other, the desirability of gaining a 'tow' from a faster machine was absolute. At first, I was unaware of the significance of such an effect, then, one day very early in my career, I was barrelling on with the HWM when a Ferrari driver chopped in front of me. It turned out that *he* was trying to lose someone else from his slipstream; by making me the meat in the sandwich he quite rightly felt that he could get away from his threatening rival. Anyway, I immediately realised that by tucking in close behind a faster car I could hang another 500 rpm on to the HWM – in top gear! Luckily in the case of that old plodder (it boasted the uninspired Alta 4-cylinder engine) the extra revs hardly threatened its reliability. What they did result in was an extra 14 mph down the straight, which I can tell you made a lot of difference to me!

I really had very little chance of winning in those days but if I managed to finish fourth or fifth a lot of people would come up and say, 'Well done, that was a great drive'. And you knew you had done well because you had beaten all the other 'no-hopers'. I don't think I ever did win a big race with the HWM. On the Continent my best effort with it was to finish third in a Formula One race (and the HWM was an F2 car, remember) at Bari. But that was a real bonus.

Later, after Vanwall pulled out and I elected to drive for Rob Walker, I found myself once again struggling with cars which, because they were not the latest available, often left something to be desired. My ambition, therefore, was to beat the works teams as frequently as possible. In 1959 Rob's Cooper was, except for the gearbox, very similar to the factory machines, and in fact by fitting an Italian transmission system we felt we might even have an advantage. As things turned out, the gearbox had basic manufacturing faults in terms of both materials and technique which were not spotted until too late and, naturally, the thing kept breaking. I would lead races comfortably, then everything would grind to a halt. Now that was pretty frustrating, but there was never an occasion when I thought, 'This is no good, I might as well tell Rob I'm packing it in to drive for Ferrari'. Similarly, in 1961 when we were running a $1\frac{1}{2}$-litre, 4-cylinder Lotus-Climax, we suffered from a lack of power. I could usually beat the British works cars and I could nearly always beat the Porsches, but getting the better of the V6 Ferraris, which had about 190 bhp compared to our 150 bhp, was something else again. I did manage to beat them at Monaco and again at the Nurburgring, and those were tremendously satisfying victories. But I was driving just as hard elsewhere, even at places like Spa and Monza on high-speed circuits where we didn't have a hope in hell of winning.

There was only one time in my career when I did not try as hard as I could have done and that was at Zandvoort in 1960. The reason I departed from my normal approach was because I had been receiving a lot of criticism for being a car breaker. We had had a lot of failures, particularly during the previous year, as I've mentioned, and people were putting this down to my driving. If I had a half lap lead and then the car broke, the suggestion that I had overstressed it was perhaps a logical one. The same thing would happen, indeed does happen, today. The point is that I knew that I did not break cars, and I think Rob knew as well, but the criticism worried me. Every time I jumped into the lead I thought, 'God, if it fails now they're going to say it was my fault'.

For the Dutch Grand Prix I decided to change my tactics. I explained the position to Rob and told him that for once I would not attempt to lead in the early stages. I would hold back and hopefully pull out and pass whoever *was* in front with a couple of laps to go. I think Rob was a bit surprised at this but he said, 'OK, if that's what you want to do, go ahead'. I had been fastest in practice so I was fairly confident that things would work out, even though this style of racing was not the one I honestly felt was right. At the start Jack Brabham rushed ahead and I sat on his tail. All went well for sixteen laps until suddenly Jack's Cooper dislodged one of the concrete slabs which marked the inside of the corners. It came at me like a missile and hit one of my front wheels; the tyre burst and, after a very hairy moment, I was left to limp to the pits. The whole wheel had broken under the impact and it took three minutes to change it. Thereafter I went flat out to make up as much time as I could, finally ending up fourth after breaking the lap record. My change of tactics had backfired well and truly, costing me the race. I had driven even harder after my stop than I would have if I had been leading the race and the car never missed a beat. It was a race full of irony and I soon reverted to my old, realistic style of grabbing the lead as early as possible and winning by as big a margin as I could. I think there are drivers today, like Jones and Villeneuve, who race in much the same way but there are others who don't and there are some top names who, if they are not behind the wheel of an obvious worldbeater, appear to lose heart. As far as I was concerned being thoroughly beaten in one race made me all the more determined in the next; I owed that much to myself, to my team and, particularly in the early days, to my country too.

Sadly, drivers sometimes now do not seem able to keep a sense of proportion; their priorities, and their loyalties, have become a trifle mixed up. I suspect that they underestimate the importance of the public, the importance of *their* image *to* the public and of the image of the sport itself.

Look, there's nothing wrong in promoting oneself, and hoping for more money. When I was waving to the crowd in the early fifties (sometimes to non-existent people!) I was doing that for Stirling Moss, in an effort to impress the organisers with my appeal and consequent value to them. I wanted them to invite me back next year and to pay me twice as much because I was such a popular guy! But at the same time I felt a great national pride in becoming reasonably well-known in Europe and elsewhere. Remember, in World Championship racing, or perhaps I should say in Grand Prix racing, Britain had done nothing at that time. Before the war, ERAs, driven by men like Raymond Mays and Prince Bira, had done well in 'Voiturette' racing, but the really big events were forever being won by foreign machinery - Mercedes Benz or Auto Union, Alfa Romeo or Ferrari. Nor, apart from Dick Seaman in the thirties, had British drivers broken into the big-time in motor sport. When I started racing abroad there were Ascari, Farina, Fangio, Gonzales, Villoresi, Taruffi, Fagioli and before that there had been Nuvolari, Caracciola, Lang, von Brauchitsch and Rosemeyer. Seaman, driving for Mercedes Benz, had been the exception as far as Britain was concerned but by the fifties we had no-one in the top flight at all.

Now, my formative school years had been spent during the war. I was probably not aware of it at the time, but I think the war years, with Britain overcoming enormous adversity, influenced me a great deal. I have always been very pro-British, and I suppose the wartime experience is partly why. As a British driver, to enter an arena in which as a nation we had so far been unsuccessful made me especially keen to do well. I wanted to drive a British car, but most of all I wanted to go as hard as I could in an effort to prove a point. Green cars (green has always been the official British racing colour) were a rare sight on foreign race tracks and I think the overseas public sympathised with our plight. But dawdling round at the back just hoping to finish seemed pointless to me. Sympathy would surely turn to derision. No, my idea was to go as fast as possible, to show that even if we couldn't win British cars and drivers could still make their mark.

Of course, there came a time when to be able to mix with the big boys in Formula One I *had* to drive a foreign car, there was simply nothing available in this country. But even then, having bought a 250F Maserati, I did paint it green. And later, when the Maserati factory asked me to join them, although naturally the car was in the entrant's Italian red, I had a Union Jack on the side. If I won, no matter for whom I was driving, our national anthem was played, and that was particularly pleasing, especially perhaps in Germany. Later, I believe it was the car's entrant for whom the anthem was played, but now it's been changed back so as to denote the driver's nationality. It's important that the organisers get it right, too - ask Alan Jones. After a disappointing first half to the 1979 season, Alan suddenly started to win race after race. He was victorious in the German, Austrian, Dutch and Canadian Grands Prix and the race organisers were often foxed as to what they should play. 'Waltzing Matilda' alternated with 'God Save The Queen', and it was not, I'm told, until his third victory that the correct tune of 'Advance Australia Fair' was played. By then Alan was probably carrying round the correct recording himself!

Over the past two decades, our own anthem has been heard a lot at race circuits. When I was starting, it was hardly ever heard, except in Britain itself and only then at minor races. When I started winning I'm not sure that every organiser even had a record of the National Anthem in his files; but they were soon made to put right the omission.

The decision to purchase the Maserati was actually made for me, behind my back if you like, by my manager and my father. I was abroad at the time, or rather I was on the high seas returning from holiday in the liner Queen Mary. One day I got a call on the radio-telephone to tell me the car had been bought – with my money! It was a big step to take, and had I been at home I suppose I might even then have tried to avoid going to a foreign manufacturer. But it was too late, the deal had been done and there's no doubt whatsoever that the decision was the correct one at the time. I wanted desperately to drive for Britain, and for a short time I had persevered with my own 'special' called a Cooper-Alta. But this was a complete disaster, and by 1954 I had resigned myself to the fact that if I wanted to 'run with the big boys' I had to do so behind the wheel of a non-British car.

Ken Gregory, my manager, had actually tried to get me into the crack Mercedes-Benz team. Mercedes were making a comeback in '54 and there was no doubt that they were going to wipe the floor with everything else. Fangio had already signed and the grapevine told us that the design of the car was going to be very advanced indeed. Not surprisingly, they told Ken that I needed more experience. 'If your boy is as good as you say,' they told him, 'Let him prove it in a decent car. Then we'll see.'

In an indirect way, then, it was Mercedes who prompted the purchase of the Maser and luckily I did manage to do well enough in 1954 to convince them that I could indeed win races for them. Most people, incidentally, think that it was through my drive in the Italian Grand Prix that I landed my place with Mercedes for 1955. Not so. Although I went well at Monza, leading the race by a long way until the oil tank split, the offer from Mercedes had already been made. It was not the events of Monza that influenced them as much as those of Bremgarten - the venue of the Swiss Grand Prix - two weeks earlier. The Bremgarten circuit was one of the most challenging and difficult in Europe and just the sort of 'real road' course that I loved best. Normally, I couldn't have hoped to compete with the Mercs but on the first day of practice it rained cats and dogs. The wet tended to wipe out the power advantage of the Mercedes cars and needless to say I had a good old go with the Maserati. I was astonished, nevertheless, when the times were issued; I was fastest, quicker even than Fangio.

The next day, with the road dry, sanity returned and I ended up third on the grid behind Gonzales and Fangio and ahead of Trintignant and Kling. But as a single piece of driving over a full-blooded Grand Prix track, I still rate that first day's practice lap as perhaps the best and most significant performance of my entire career. It astounded me, and it certainly seemed to impress Mercedes, who almost immediately said, 'OK, let's talk terms for next year's season'.

I include this to put the record straight, and to show how even the Mercedes team could, at certain times, be beaten. But even though I enjoyed my best season by far during 1955, winning the British Grand Prix and finishing second to Fangio in the World Championship, I still yearned to be part of a British set-up.

Nothing was on a par with Mercedes during '55 - not even Ferrari could keep up. The German cars won five of the six Grands Prix (yes, that's all there were that year, a legacy of the Le Mans disaster) and at Aintree they finished first, second, third, fourth, with myself in front. When this particular race is ever discussed the same old question is always broached - did Fangio let me win, or did I beat him fair and square? To this day, I do not know. Obviously, I was very keen to win in front of a British crowd and Fangio knew how much a home victory would mean to me. And I'm sure if I asked him that same question today he would say, 'You were first, and I was second, and that's all there is to it'. It was, nevertheless, the only time I finished ahead of the maestro that year, and the doubt lingers. I'm certain that if we had been racing in Argentina that day Fangio would have moved heaven and earth to make sure he won. Just as Italians go better at Monza, and Frenchmen come alive at Monte Carlo, so Fangio became almost superhuman in Buenos Aires – he won the Argentinian GP four years on the trot! By the same token, however, it is possible that Moss was that much more on the boil at Aintree and I know I would have defended my position like mad if Juan Manuel had tried to pass.

Team tactics at Mercedes were straightforward; we were expected to build up a thirty second lead and then hold station. Once the thirty second margin had been achieved, Neubauer would in fact hold out a signal reading 'REG', short for regulari. In effect this meant 'hold position', telling me that I must not race Fangio, but just stay in his wheeltracks – assuming I was able to. In theory, if I had been in front at that point, with Fangio behind, the same rule would have applied – he would not have challenged me and I would have won. As it turned out that situation was never put to the test. Although Mercedes never insisted on me being Number Two, Fangio, many years older than me and current World Champion, was clearly the senior driver. I was the new boy in the team and no way was I going to mess things up by trying to dice with the established genius.

In the two races previous to Aintree, at Spa and at Zandvoort, we ran virtually nose to tail: in Belgium I finished eight seconds behind and in Holland I was hard up behind Fangio to the end. At Aintree Mercedes entered four cars for the British Grand Prix. I started from pole position with Fangio alongside me and Kling and Taruffi in the second row. Only Jean Behra and his Maserati could get in amongst the silver cars in practice, the Frenchman starting from the outside of the front row. I remember the race being a bit of a hotch-potch. First I would lead, then Fangio would come by, then I would repass. I remember Behra chasing us hard over the first few laps, but once he had retired there could be no doubt that Mercedes were going to win again. Then towards the end there came a point where I was in the lead as we came up on some back-markers. I remember passing one of these tail-enders just before a corner and leaving him between myself and Fangio. I thought, 'This is great, now I'm going to go like hell'. I really tried everything I knew and indeed from that moment in the race Fangio did not manage to pass me again. On the last corner I did pull over to give him a clear run, but I kept my right foot flat on the boards and I didn't really think he could overtake on the short piece of straight up to the flag. Oddly enough, although Fangio and I had a huge lead once Behra had gone, the REG board was never hung out. Or if it was, I never saw it.... In the end, Mercedes took the first four places, with myself just one-fifth of a second ahead of the great Juan Manuel.

At the end of 1955 Mercedes pulled out of racing - they had proved their point - and I was again left without a drive. There were two options open to me: either I could do a deal with Ferrari or Maserati, or I could return to the old business of making the best of what British constructors had to offer. In the end I did both. In Grand Prix races I drove for Maserati but elsewhere, in non-championship Formula One races where Maserati were not competing, I was anxious to have a go in the Vanwall.

By this time Tony Vandervell's team was really beginning to look threatening and when I took the car to victory in the International Trophy at Silverstone things were definitely looking up. Unfortunately, due to my contractual obligations to Maserati, I did not race the Vanwall again in 1956 but there was never any doubt for whom I should drive the following year. I signed with them at the end of October and stayed for two seasons - until Tony Vandervell's health failed, in fact, and the team pulled out of serious contention. These were significant years for Britain and although the Championship continued to elude me, I did help to make a British team the best in the world. In 1958 the World Constructors' Championship was introduced and it was entirely right that Vanwall should have been the first winner. Thus Britain had world motor racing champions on two fronts: the driver in Mike Hawthorn (driving for Ferrari) and the car in the Vanwall with its three British drivers (Tony Brooks, Stuart Lewis-Evans and myself).

I am reminded at this point of another feature of bygone

years which involved a form of loyalty – driver changes. Quite often in Grand Prix racing a top driver would take over his team-mate's car after his own had run into trouble. It was a tactic I and many others employed both successfully and legitimately. For instance, at Spa and Reims in 1956 I took over Francesco Perdisa's Maserati and we finished third and fifth respectively. Then at Aintree in 1957, after my own Vanwall began to run roughly while leading, I was able to take over from Tony Brooks and win the race. Tony was unwell during that event and was happy to swop cars with me.

Our win was the first for a British car in a World Championship Grand Prix and as such it constituted a landmark in racing history. But it could not have been achieved under today's rules. The current regulations do not allow more than one driver per car, which I think is a great shame. The spectators are thus denied the spectacle of a number one driver carving his way through the field at the wheel of his team-mate's machine. Indeed sometimes they are denied seeing him at all; if a start-line shunt causes Scheckter or Jones to retire, then that's the end of their race.

In the fifties, though, driver changes were commonplace and they added to the excitement. When a driver signed for a team he did so knowing that unless he was seen to be the 'number one' he might be asked to hand over his car at any time. And in nearly every case they were willing to do so for the sake of both the team and its lead driver. I remember a time at Rouen, racing for Aston Martin, when Peter Collins insisted that I take his car instead of my own. My car had disc brakes which were giving trouble whereas his were fitted with the older but more reliable drums. He knew that his car was better than mine and said so. On another occasion, in the Italian Grand Prix at Monza, Peter handed over his Ferrari to Fangio after the maestro's car had broken its steering. Collins himself had a chance of taking the title that year, but it was typical of his unselfish attitude that he offered his car to his team leader so that the points could be shared. It was the final GP of the season and by finishing second (to me!) Fangio clinched his fourth Championship.

Even as late as 1961, my last full year, I was well aware of the usefulness of jumping into another driver's cockpit. At Monza I still stood an outside chance of pinching the driver's title from one of the Ferrari drivers. Throughout the year I had driven for Rob Walker who, as a private owner, was clearly not able to give me quite the advantages of a works team. His Lotus 18s were always that tiny bit adrift, in terms of speed and handling, of the factory's Lotus 21s, which boasted revised suspension and a smoother bodyline. At a flat-out circuit like Monza that streamlined shape was likely to pay dividends - and how I coveted the works cars with their wind-cheating profile.

Team Lotus themselves had a vested interest in my performance because if I could win the Championship so could they - the name Lotus was obviously common to all our cars. I was taken by surprise, nevertheless, when Innes Ireland, then the Team Lotus number one driver, offered to exchange cars with me the night before the race. I hadn't even practised the works car, but overnight the works entry was fitted with the top body panel bearing my race number for me to drive while Innes took over my car complete with his original number. The key factor in all this was that the factory car was equipped with inboard front springs and boasted a smaller frontal area, all of which made it appreciably faster through the air than my earlier model. In the race, poor Innes retired with a cracked chassis - my chassis! - while I went out near the end with a broken wheel bearing. But I had been running second until that point and had I finished in that position I would have been able to contest the Championship over the remaining two rounds. As it was, Phil Hill clinched the title at Monza after his team-mate, Wolfgang von Trips, had been tragically killed.

Countless versions of 'musical chairs' amongst the team drivers helped keep interest during my era and also said a lot for team spirit. I wonder now, if the rules permitted it, just how many 'number two' drivers would stand for being requested to give up their seats half-way through a race.

Having been part of major works teams for four years (years in which, frankly, I was expected to win every time) I think I was a bit relieved to find myself subsequently driving for privateers like Rob Walker or my own family team, the British Racing Partnership. The Grand Prix cars I raced until my enforced retirement were invariably British and, indeed, from this time on British machinery was to be on top. On the other hand, the pressure of being the number one driver in a high-powered factory outfit was eased. Whenever I drove Rob's cars, or BRP's cars, I saw myself once again adopting the role of the underdog, one I have always enjoyed. If I had driven for Cooper direct, or maybe Lotus, I would perhaps have been more successful than I was. The fact is that I wasn't quite as deadly serious about motor racing as is sometimes made out. I preferred to do it the hard way, to pose myself an extra challenge. That way victory, when it came, was always that much sweeter. Earlier in my career, British cars had no chance at all. Then, when they did have a chance, I was delighted to race for a big factory team, to put Britain firmly on the map. But by 1959 British machinery was winning almost everything and I was happier to carry the flag of the private owner.

If I had really wanted to win the World Championship I would have driven for Ferrari every year. Like all teams Ferrari had off years, but you could depend on them bouncing back to scoop the pool the following season. Their drivers won the world title in 1952, 1953, 1956, 1958 and 1961. They were always the cars to beat in Formula One racing, their performance the yardstick by which other teams could judge themselves.

There were two reasons why I did not drive for Ferrari. One I have explained, being that of national pride. The other was that of personal pride, of conscience. Early in my career I was once badly let down by Ferrari and I swore then never to race one of his cars in a Grand Prix. I did drive various types of Ferrari, Grand Touring cars and so on, but it was always for private owners, never the works team. The only time I did get near to racing a works Ferrari, at Bari in 1951, I arrived to find the Commendatore had changed his mind.

What happened was this. I had been driving HWMs with very limited success, but going well enough to get myself known. One day Ferrari himself rang up and asked if I would like to drive one of his cars in the Bari Grand Prix. Naturally I was flattered and agreed readily. Here was a great opportunity to prove my worth. The Ferrari I was due to drive was a new one, a 2½-litre prototype, and I was looking forward immensely to comparing it with the poor old HWM. I told my father who was as thrilled as I was and we jumped on an aeroplane and flew all the way down to Bari. When I got there I found the Ferrari garage and spotted my car straightaway. I climbed into the thing to get the feel of it and then up came a mechanic. He wanted to know what I was doing. I introduced myself and said, 'This is my car'. He replied, 'I'm sorry, this car is for Piero Taruffi'. I was amazed. I told him there had to be a mistake, that Ferrari had invited me personally. But no, it soon became quite clear that he had changed his mind and that Taruffi was to drive it after all.

I don't particularly blame Ferrari for preferring Taruffi to me because, I'm sure, at that time he was a better and more experienced driver. But to have asked me to drive, get down there and then leave me dangling was unforgivable as far as I was concerned. I vowed there and then never to drive for Ferrari, and I never did.

The Ferrari I finally raced at Bari was a 2-litre belonging to David Murray. Understanding my predicament David very kindly lent me his own car which I promptly shunted! It had a central accelerator layout which I wasn't used to and I went off the road. It was an ironic experience. I had gone to Bari as a works Ferrari driver, ready to pulverise the opposition in a brand new model. I ended up being shunned by the team and crashing a car lent by a friend!

Well, that was the one and only time I raced a Ferrari single-seater, but I must reveal that in 1961, ten years later almost to the day, Ferrari again approached me. He invited me down to Modena, took me to lunch and was very, very gracious towards me. He said, 'Look, tell me what you want and I will build you a car that will win the Championship'.

I thought, well, it had been ten years since that fiasco at Bari and things had changed. Britain was well on top generally and it seemed to me that no disloyalty would be involved if, for once, I drove a Grand Prix Ferrari. So I said 'All right, I will drive one of your cars, but it must be painted either in Rob Walker blue (which by then had become as symbolically British as genuine British racing green) or in the pale green of the British Racing Partnership. It will have a Union Jack on the side and it will be run from the UK. You will supply the car and all spares and pay for its maintenance.' To my surprise Ferrari agreed to all this and for the 1962 Grand Prix season I was all set to race whatever his latest model might have been.

All these plans came to naught because of my Easter Monday crash at Goodwood, but interestingly Ferrari did provide a car for me at one race, the International Trophy in May. By this time I was out for the count in the Atkinson Morley Hospital, but the car was handed over to the British Racing Partnership with a pale green stripe painted down its red nose. At that time BRP were being supported and sponsored by UDT-Laystall, and so in the programme it went down as an official UDT entry. But it was the car intended for me, supplied personally by Enzo Ferrari. Innes Ireland actually drove it at Silverstone where I believe he led on the opening lap and finally finished fourth.

After that, when it became clear that my recovery was likely to be a long and tedious affair, the car was handed back. I'm sure that BRP would have loved to continue running the thing but obviously Ferrari himself regarded the deal as one between two men rather than between two teams. Ironically, Ferrari had a very lean time of it in 1962, being completely outclassed by the latest V8 designs from BRM, Lotus-Climax, Lola-Climax and Cooper-Climax, not forgetting the flat-8 Porsche. He relied on his 1961 cars to pull him through and this proved a great mistake. The cars had swept all before them the previous year, but such was the progress made by the British teams over the winter that not even Phil Hill, the current champion and leading Ferrari driver, could do much about it. Had I driven a Ferrari that year, however, I might have quite enjoyed the experience. I would have tried my damndest to beat the works Ferraris even if I could not have kept up with the likes of Jimmy Clark in his Lotus or Graham Hill in his BRM. It could have been one hell of a year. We shall never know.

MIKE HAILWOOD

Patriotism has never played a major part in my career and I can't honestly say I ever felt that I was 'racing for Britain'. During my motorcycling career I would have been delighted if someone had asked me to ride a British worldbeater. But there just weren't any! Foreign bikes dominated the top-class scene and so I rode for the Italians, the Japanese and the East Germans. If I wanted to win I had to do this – and it's just the same today. In the early days I used to race British bikes, such as Nortons and AJs, because there wasn't anything else. But as soon as I could get onto something better I did – and so did everyone else.

Strangely enough, there has never been the same kind of national fervour in bike racing as there is in the car world. I suppose the Marlboro Transatlantic Trophy does whip up the old patriotic passions these days, but in my day the rivalry existed more between factories and individuals than between countries. The Italian MVs were painted red (the Italian national racing colour) but then so were the Hondas and other non-Italian bikes.

Car racing is different. There has always been the chance for British cars to do well. It was a terrific time for British motorsport back in the fifties and sixties when Stirling was driving and Vanwall, Cooper, Lotus and BRM finally managed to overcome the might of crack foreign teams like Ferrari and Maserati. In bike racing I'm afraid things worked the other way round. Once the Japanese entered the arena the British bikes just didn't stand a chance.

Frankly, loyalty meant and does mean more to me than patriotism – loyalty to teams, loyalty to sponsors, loyalty to fans. I think that I was always considered to be a loyal type of bloke, and I know I tried to be because for me both motorbike and car racing were just another way of earning a living, and I think that any employer has every right to expect those working for him to remain faithful and not let him down.

I always had a good relationship with my sponsors – Matchbox, Brooke Bond, Oxo and Yardley, companies which are still very loyal to me today. I can only remember one occasion when I had problems. Brooke Bond decided to bring along some of those famous TV chimpanzees to one of the races to meet me. One of the chimps (I never did find out her name!) promptly fell in love with yours truly and proceeded to smother me with soggy chimpanzee 'kisses'. Unfortunately, carried away by the emotion of the occasion, the 'kisses' turned to bites – large bites – and I had to rush off and don my Nomex overalls and face mask before I suffered serious injury!

On another occasion, at Monaco, I was somewhat surprised, but not displeased, to find a willowy blonde lady clad in driver's overalls sitting in the cockpit of my Yardley 'Mac'. I was just beginning to wonder if this was a subtle way of telling me that I had been replaced, when the Yardley people explained to me that she was a fashion model on a photographic shoot. Of course, this didn't prevent me from being the target of various scurrilous comments, particularly from Peter Mackintosh of the Constructors' Association who promptly informed everybody: 'We're happy to report that Mike's sex change operation was a huge success!'

I was also a great believer in loyalty to my team, even when things got horribly frustrating, as they did with Surtees in 1973. I remember one disastrous meeting in Austria that year. I think I must have only done about four laps in practice, and three of those were on the back of the tow truck! We had more mechanical problems than I care to remember, so I figured I just had to be philosophical about the whole thing. Throwing a mood wasn't going to help matters, so I just tucked a good detective novel into my overalls and set off for a read in the cornfields at the beginning of each session. I got through an awful lot of books that weekend!

At another race that same year (I think it was the French) Carlos (Pace) and I had what *we* thought were some good ideas about modifications for the nose of the Surtees. John wasn't able to make the first two practice sessions for some reason, so we coerced the mechanics into trying out our 'mods'. Now neither Carlos nor I were renowned for our 'technical' ability and 'Big John' had pretty set ideas when it came to driver suggestions for 'technical' improvements! When he arrived and saw what had been done to the car he was furious and insisted that the 'revolutionary' Hailwood/Pace ideas be scrapped – although the cars' performances had in fact improved. A couple of races later we arrived at the circuit to find our cars with these splendid modifications – our modifications – but, of course, now the brainchild of one J. Surtees Esq!

I can't honestly sympathise with drivers like Niki and James for walking out on their jobs the way they did in 1979. I can understand that they were both desperately frustrated by the situation but I simply cannot condone the way they went about solving matters. If they had been competing for nothing or buying their drives, they might well have been entitled to quit just when they felt like it, as I did in 1965. But they weren't. Both of them had signed contracts for huge amounts of money. If I were Bernie Ecclestone of Brabham or Peter Warr of Walter Wolf Racing, I think I would probably have sued them until the cows came home. It all ties in with what I said earlier about handing people a bag of gold *before* they've even stepped into a car. It's diabolical behaviour, a 'prima donna' attitude which I find totally inexcusable on the race track or off it. It suggests that motor racing is a false and shallow business, a business in which normal standards of personal reliability and dedication do not exist.

Just think of the fans - enthusiasts who had booked those expensive grandstand seats at Silverstone for the British Grand Prix and were expecting to see their hero, James Hunt, in action. They had cheered him at Silverstone in 1977 when he thrashed everybody in his McLaren, and they had roared him on at Brands the previous year on his way to winning the World Championship, when he chased and beat Niki Lauda fair and square (only to be controversially, and in my view unfairly, disqualified later). In 1979 they had had to commit themselves in advance to see their man, and he wasn't there. The public knew he was going through a bad patch, but they would have cheered him on just the same.

Retiring gracefully at the end of a successful - or even unsuccessful - career is one thing. No-one would have blamed either James or Niki for packing it in after the Watkins Glen race in October. Look at Jackie Stewart who made the perfectly timed ending to a perfect career. He knew exactly how to handle things. Motor racing is a notoriously fickle sport (I can certainly vouch for that!) and most people do have their ups and downs, that is the very nature of the sport, but no-one ever knows just what is round the next corner. Okay, so neither of their cars were going well, but fortunes change, and both guys had been in the sport long enough to be only too well aware of that.

I can see that James, having a similar outlook on life to mine, probably found that Grand Prix racing just wasn't fun any more. I can understand that because I can remember my own frustrations in the seventies. And I'm sure things must have got worse when 'ground effect' technology took its grip and rendered the driver less important than the designer. I must admit that in my day the driver *did* still count for something, you did influence your own destiny.

Niki's decision is much harder to fathom. He has always been a very deep and complex character. I know because he used to share my flat for a time in the early seventies. He was very single-minded then, and we used to call him 'Little Hitler'. He would get very irate and thump the table, demanding 'Ve vill have dinner at six o'clock'! He couldn't cope with the idea that we were all intending to go off for a few drinks before the meal and had no intention of dining much before ten o'clock. In other words he found it difficult to adapt to our rules. I never did understand at the time what his ambitions were. He was still driving in Formula Two, still very much a 'learner' as far as the big time was concerned. Much later it became obvious that he had set his heart on becoming World Champion.

Niki always did things his way, so perhaps we shouldn't be surprised at the way he walked out. He'd already done it once before, after all, when he declined to race for Ferrari in 1977 in the last two races of the season in North America. He'd just won the World Championship at Monza and he had a nice fat contract with Brabham for the 1978 season sitting in his pocket. He didn't like the treatment meted out to him by Ferrari so he just walked out and refused to race in Canada and the States. Maybe Bernie Ecclestone should have seen the warning lights then. Knowing Niki, I'm sure he felt justified in that introspective way of his, but I found it a very disloyal way to behave. What about all those fans in North America who were deprived of their opportunity of seeing the World Champion? And what about the sponsors who had supported him through his Championship year?

I can just imagine how those Brabham mechanics felt in Canada last year. They had worked long and hard to build their new Cosworth-powered car for Niki to drive at the very race meeting at which he announced his withdrawal. He literally turned his back on the whole business after a few laps in that new car, walked out on those hard-working mechanics, his sponsors, and the public. Even Bernie Ecclestone couldn't believe it.

Maybe Niki could have won in that car. His team-mate Nelson Piquet certainly impressed in it in both North American races. Niki could have gone out covered in glory. He could have done justice to all the hard work put in by the Brabham mechanics, designers and engineers, and he could have repaid the faith and money invested in him by Ecclestone, Parmalat and all the other sponsors. I know which way I would have chosen.

When I was racing I simply wouldn't have dared to walk out on everything. In those latter days I wasn't wild about the atmosphere in Formula One but I never thought 'I must get out. This game's no fun any more'. In some ways the more frustrating Grand Prix racing became the harder I tried and winning, or attempting to win, became the only thing that mattered - I certainly wasn't in it for enjoyment!

Even if things had become twice as dangerous, I think I would have stuck with it. I really believe that in racing the likelihood of breaking one's neck *can* be controlled. It's like riding at the Isle of Man. No-one in their right mind goes flat out there because if you fall off you're in real trouble. The technique with the Island is to put in as many laps as possible before racing starts, learn the course (over 40 miles long, remember), figure out where you can afford to go fast, and then race as hard as you can under the circumstances. On sections where one mistake would have you smashing into a brick wall, you roll it off a fraction. In car racing the same applies. You don't have to put your life on the line unnecessarily. Loyalty to the cause doesn't extend beyond loyalty to one's life!

I can understand that Niki felt bitter about Ferrari ever since the 1976 Grand Prix at Fuji. He had clawed his way back after his horrific accident at the Ring despite shocking pain and disfigurement. He was out to regain his title in spite of everything. Come the final race in Japan, Niki had to finish in the first six to be sure of the Championship. What happened?

The race was flagged off in atrocious conditions and Lauda

retired after two laps judging the track to be too dangerous for racing. Hunt finished third and snatched his title from him. The Italian Press tore Niki to pieces. He was guilty of 'cowardice and disloyalty'. He had a right to feel bitter.

He made a very brave decision that day, risking not just the pundits' scorn but the loss of the title he so much wanted, and it seems that Ferrari never quite forgave him for it. But what a different situation he found himself in a year later. He chose to withdraw from the North American races not because of any fear of the danger but to teach Ferrari a lesson, I suppose. How strange that someone who can show such physical and moral courage can behave in such a way. However, I understand how Niki must have felt at Fuji. I remember all too vividly just what it is like to race cars or bikes under diabolical conditions. Having an accident was most definitely *not* my idea of having fun. I reckoned I was doing everyone a favour if I backed off and stayed on the road rather than drive over my head to prove what a lunatic I could be. And if the conditions were so bad that retirement seemed like a sensible route, fair enough.

This was the case at Spa in 1966 after I left MV and was riding for Honda. I had won the 250 race from Phil Read and was confident that I could take the 500 event, the Belgian Grand Prix, an event I had won four years in a row. I had won the 500cc World Championship four years in succession, but in 1966 by the time we arrived at Spa Agostini was leading the points table, with my Rhodesian team-mate Jim Redman second and myself third. I had to do well in Belgium to stand a chance of making it five titles in a row. I must say I felt reasonably confident.

Things went according to plan to start with and I built up a long lead. But then down came the rain, as it only can at Spa, and I literally could not see where I was going. Conditions were appalling. The circuit was swamped. Jim fell off and broke his arm and I thought, 'This is ridiculous. We're not racing any more, just hanging on for survival'. So, despite my lead (and I think I could probably have won the race by pushing the bike home) and despite my eagerness to win the 500 Championship for the fifth time, I cruised into the pits and called it quits. I don't think I have ever felt so relieved.

Agostini won the race and went on to take the title, his first 500cc Championship which he thoroughly deserved. I finished runner-up. But I have no regrets whatsoever about my decision that day at Spa.

Obviously, any professional competitor has an obligation to his entrant and sponsor, not to mention his fans, to give of his best. But in the final analysis there is only one person who can weigh up the odds in a given situation. Ninety-nine times out of a hundred any racer worth his salt will go like mad in an effort to win, but on that hundreth occasion, when the risks cannot be justified, then I believe he must be allowed to 'follow his nose' and jack it in if he feels that strongly about it, *without* any outside pressure. There comes a time in every racing man's career when he thinks to himself, 'This is stupid'. But believe me, it takes real courage to pursue the honest course, to back off the throttle, to give up the unequal struggle.

4 Technology and technique

STIRLING MOSS

Looking hard at Grand Prix racing as it is now, I can see that in one area at least, perhaps two, technology has run away with itself. I am all for technical development, but only where the racing itself will benefit. Here's the dilemma. Thanks to some marvellous work by the technicians at Goodyear and Michelin (and earlier, at Firestone and Dunlop), the modern racing tyre offers the kind of grip which my contemporaries and I never even dreamt about. But *because* of this, driving techniques, circuit design and, most especially, the relative performance of the various Grand Prix teams have all been affected in what I believe to be a detrimental manner.

In my day tyres were fairly primitive – startlingly narrow and made of 'hard' rubber. I can certainly recognise that as power output goes up, which it has, the amount of rubber you need on the road goes up too. Advancement, however, is one thing, mutation is another. Today's racing tyres are a bizarre parody of their road-going counterparts, creating freak effects which I say are out of place even in the astringent and esoteric arena of Formula One. If the rules encouraged engines of 12-litre capacity there would be an outcry. Silly, irresponsible and totally pointless, the critics would wail. In my view, 20-inch wide 'gumballs' are equally silly, irresponsible and pointless and their continued use has changed the face of the sport I knew and loved.

There's a paradox here. On the one hand, today's tyres offer a level of adhesion which is, frankly, out of proportion to the straight-line speed of the contemporary Grand Prix car, and on the other they are too vulnerable even for the specially-built tracks on which they run. When I was racing, punctures were virtually unknown, and if you did get one it was because you had somehow driven over a huge nail. Today, these great soft, sticky jobs that pass for high-performance tyres can be punctured by small stones.

Occasionally we suffered from tyres wearing out – they literally wouldn't last the race before all the rubber was scrubbed away, and on even rarer occasions would throw a tread. But these problems we would find out about in practice and either use bigger wheels, by which I mean wheels with a larger diameter, to keep the temperature down, or we would plan a pit-stop so that the wheels could be changed. To make an unscheduled stop because of tyre failure was almost unheard of.

Nowadays, it seems you are lucky to escape without being forced to change at least one wheel during a race, either through puncturing or through the rubber compound overheating and 'going off'. That expression was not around in my day and I'm told it means that your lovely super-adhesive rubber suddenly loses all its grip. It's an effect that I was not accustomed to, and nor is it something that I can readily understand. Indeed, I am surprised that modern Grand Prix teams, with all their massive financial involvement, tolerate such an alarmingly unpredictable situation.

Of course, the development of sticky synthetic compounds and the staggering growth in wheel rim width, coupled with the introduction of wings and skirts, has meant that cornering speeds have risen to a level which simply could not have been anticipated twenty years ago. Fair enough, but speeds like this do bring drawbacks – safety precautions have had to become far more elaborate, often at the expense of the spectator's view. Catch fencing, Armco barriers, debris fencing, run-off areas – they have all had to be introduced or improved, at vast cost, to allow for the fact that today's racing cars are liable to fly off at 150 mph on a bend which I might have taken at 105.

I've made no secret of the fact that to me the ultimate form of motor sport is genuine road racing. I'm all for circuits running through towns, complete with drains and kerbstones and curious cambers. (In Portugal and Italy we used to race over tram lines!) These were circuits which became circuits only in the early hours of race-day morning when someone would drive round in a lorry chucking out straw bales. Well, that kind of venue doesn't work now because the modern Grand Prix cars can't cope with it – they go too fast round corners on tyres which cannot stand up to the pounding of an 'ordinary' road. I appreciate that 'road racing' of a sort still takes place at Long Beach and at Monte Carlo, but the road surfaces at both circuits are specially laid down with the cambers lessened and the drains levelled off, and the whole length of the track is lined with steel or concrete. When I raced at Monaco I would expect to bounce off a kerb if I made a mistake, or if the error was bad enough I might have anticipated hitting a wall. Alberto Ascari went into the sea and so did Paul Hawkins – and they both got away with it! I'm not entirely convinced that bouncing off a steel barrier is preferable to hitting a kerb or a wall or even diving into the Mediterranean, but I do see that the speeds currently achieved through corners make barriers of this sort highly desirable and I can certainly appreciate the need to protect the spectators.

Yet, what is being proved or achieved by such high cornering speeds? Does the onlooker feel he is getting more for his money today when he sees Alan Jones swoop round a hairpin at 60 instead of tolerating me at 40? I suspect he does not. In my view the amazing road-holding properties of modern Grand Prix cars tend to make the whole thing less spectacular. The most exciting thing I ever saw in motor racing was Froilan Gonzales fighting full-blooded, opposite lock slides driving the 1951 4½-litre Ferrari. I suppose by today's standards he wasn't going all that quickly, but it was still pretty fast and the point is that it looked absolutely fantastic. Now, of course, the cars are cornering at maybe twice Gonzales' rate but frankly they don't look even half as dramatic. And you can be sure that if drivers *do* find themselves adopting the same 'attitude angles' in a corner as was commonplace in the fifties, winding on the same degree of opposite lock, then they are totally out of control and about to dive into the catch fencing!

Thinking about cornering speeds, it's interesting to remember that going flat out down the straight GP cars of the past were as quick, or nearly so, as today's F1 cars. In fact, some were even quicker. Today's huge tyres tend to have a massively impairing effect on top speed by virtue of their drag. Back in the early fifties, 4½-litre and 1½-litre supercharged F1 cars like the Ferrari and the Alfa Romeo 159 were clocked in excess of 190 mph at Spa and Reims. Today's cars, while not quite as large in terms of engine capacity, produce more power than their forbears and should, in theory, be capable of way over 200 miles an hour. As it is, few can manage more than 185, even on the longest straights, and it is the tyres that are responsible. Sports racing machines, with their all-enveloping bodywork (not allowed in single-seater rules), are potentially faster in a straight line than a Formula One car because they possess a much lower drag factor. However you look at it, the modern F1 car is something of a freak, being slower in terms of flat out speed than both the Grand Prix vehicle of thirty years ago and its nineteen-eighties two-seater rival.

Progress has hardly been made in this area and I for one would like to see a greater discrepancy between speed on the straights and speed in corners. If this means slowing the cars down in a bend then I think that's fine, providing the skill of the driver is not diminished. By cutting rim widths I am convinced that Formula One cars will not only look more spectacular but will also be more difficult to drive. By being that much slower through corners they will help solve the ever-mounting safety problem, wiping out the need for artificial chicanes and perhaps enabling spectators to watch from closer vantage points. Narrower tyres, by virtue of possessing a much smaller 'foot-print', would also be less liable to puncturing. And if the tyre companies did their job, their products could be made sufficiently tough to be suited to proper road circuits.

As a driver, I was constantly aware of the importance of upholding the spectator value of motor racing. It matters not whether the audience is a 'live' one or whether, as is happening now, it is comprised mainly of television viewers. I've always believed that, if the racing itself cannot always be guaranteed to be close and exciting, the business of driving a racing car should at least *look* difficult. On today's tyres, I fear that to many observers it looks all too easy. Grand Prix racing, to preserve its integrity and maintain its 'entertainment quotient', needs to be seen to be as hard as I know it is. The public has to be just a bit frightened by it, I think. String a tightrope walker's wire inches above the ground and even I'd have a go – but no-one is likely to pay to watch! String it high between two buildings and it is obvious that only a real expert would venture across. I don't think the 'tightrope' of Grand Prix racing looks to be all that high off the ground at present, especially as 'safety nets' are obligatory.

I feel, too, that tyres play such a disproportionately large part in the overall performance of a racing car that the natural differential between the top drivers and the rest is unfairly disguised. Remember Nurburgring in 1957, when Fangio passed Peter Collins on one side and then Mike Hawthorn on the other to win the German Grand Prix? His was a fabulous drive and the difference in ability between him and the average midfield runner was there for all to see. In terms of time it was about fifteen seconds a lap!

Finding himself, following a pit-stop for fuel and tyres, 45 seconds behind Hawthorn and Collins, Fangio did the impossible. He caught both the Ferrari drivers within seven laps, shouldered them mercilessly out of the way to win the German Grand Prix and in doing so put the existing lap record (held by himself!) almost to shame. He forced his Maserati round the 14-mile course no fewer than 24 seconds faster than the year previously, and eight seconds better than he had achieved in practice. It was a *tour de force* which you knew had very little to do with the nimbleness of the Maserati; driving similar factory-entered cars, all 250Fs, Behra and Schell could only finish sixth and seventh. Fangio's drive that day virtually clinched his fifth and final Championship and left the racing world in no doubt that, even at the age of 46, he was still the best racing driver of the lot. It served as an example of 'sheer speed' which, paradoxically, bore only an academic relationship to miles per hour. As it happened, Fangio was lapping the Ring at over 90 mph. Today, were they to race over the same circuit, most F1 drivers would get round at an average way over 120 – but I doubt if any of them would be able to emulate the 'Old Man', not in such an obvious fashion. Fangio's performance that occasion – and on many others – was sensational, and it *looked* sensational too, because he had to drive in a different fashion from modern competitors. Throttle control, in particular, was more important because the tyres, skinny things that they were, tended to lose their grip at much lower cornering forces.

In 1979 there was a great deal of moaning and groaning amongst the top drivers over the necessity of being in the 'right' car. It seemed that unless you were 'lucky' enough to be in a Williams, a Ferrari, a Renault or perhaps a Ligier you stood very little chance of winning. 'Ground effect' bestowed insuperable advantages on certain designs, allowing a car to be cornered so fast that driver expertise was lessened. All the vehicles that year had benefited from ground effect technology, but clearly some designers approached perfection in creating the optimum levels of 'suction' where others merely produced copycat designs which fell short of what was required. By creating a partial vacuum under the car which literally sucked it to the road, it is little wonder that lap records were smashed throughout the season. The adhesive qualities of the wide tyres were suddenly given a massive boost via aerodynamic effect and the illusion of F1 cars running 'on rails' as in table-top motor racing became quite believable. I do not applaud drivers for 'going on' about the disparity between one car and another, but it is certainly true that ground effect compounded a felony already perpetrated by oversize tyres.

Clearly, today's machines have progressed to the point where even if you doubled the engine size the sophistication of the chassis would still be able to tame the power. In my day, things were different indeed. Roughly speaking, the general idea was to get the car going faster by virtue of engine development rather than via improvements in chassis and suspension. Obviously, handling was important, but really I feel it was left to the driver to cope with the roadholding, or lack of it, which is why it was so much easier then to identify the best from the rest. Coming to terms with cars which were super-fast down the straight but which didn't handle all that brilliantly was the essence of my job.

Chassis and suspension design was, in the fifties, a fairly haphazard affair. Designers recognised the need for sophistication but the end product didn't always perform exactly as anticipated. Obviously, a powerful car has always been more demanding than a slower one, but sometimes a car with a supposedly advanced chassis could be just as demanding, and vice-versa. For instance, a Cooper was always an easy car to drive. It was very competitive, and thereby very successful, but it had a forgiving nature. Its chassis design was crude, but it was effective for its era. In the sixties, as chassis construction grew steadily more sophisticated, the fortunes of Cooper declined. John Cooper and his father belonged to an earlier decade, one where improvisation and inspired guesswork did better than aerospace manufacturing techniques and computerised stress formulae. For its time, however, the Cooper was a super car. It was so easy one could almost be blasé about it. When Colin Chapman introduced his rear-engined Lotus in 1960, the writing was on the wall as far as design was concerned. His car was only marginally faster than the Cooper, but it was much more difficult to drive. To get the most out of it you had to be that much better a driver, which was fair enough. There were other cars of my period which boasted 'sophistication' but which were often dreadful to actually race at high speed. The Mercedes was difficult, and so was the Vanwall, but the 250F Maserati was fairly easy, although only in its standard form. In an effort to improve its roadholding, the Maserati factory introduced a drastically lightened and shortened version in 1958 dubbed the 'Piccolo'. This was the last of the series and by this time Maserati had run desperately short of money. The Piccolo was their last bid for glory and it proved unsuccessful. The thinking with regards to the chassis backfired and made the car not only no quicker than it had been, but also much less pleasant to drive. Like the swing-axle Ferrari of 1951, the Piccolo was a bad car in terms of the power it had to deal with. If I had had to race the Piccolo in 1958, I would have got on with it, but I wouldn't have enjoyed it. As it happened, I did race it in 1978 and 1979 in historic events and, because I was racing for pleasure and for no other reason, I eventually said to JCB Excavators, the owners, 'Thanks for everything, but I really must find a new car – this one is just too touchy!'

By and by, however, designers came to understand very much more about how a Formula One car should be built and the emphasis swung right away from power to handling, braking and roadholding. The designs are so effective, and the chassis, suspension and tyre 'tuning' that goes on throughout practice has developed into such a fine art, that in the end all the driver has to do is press the button and go. That's an exaggeration, obviously, but the fact remains that you know Andretti on the fourth row will be able to do nothing about Jones on the front row because the Lotus just isn't quite as fast as the Williams - or wasn't in 1979-80. Andretti, you see, would be unable to exploit his car in the way I was able to exploit mine. He could exploit it to the point of near maximum performance but then find the harder he tried, the worse things became. Of all the drivers, Andretti especially would recognise the futility of getting a modern F1 vehicle 'out of shape'. The more sideways it becomes, the more time will be lost through the friction of the huge tyres scrubbing against the road. Also the necessity of keeping the underside of the car 'boxed in' to produce the required suction makes bounding off kerbs another pointless exercise. If I needed to go faster I would brake later and accelerate earlier. I would endeavour to balance out a slide better, and for a longer period. Today, that technique doesn't seem to work and you can sense the frustration amongst all the top drivers. The cars of the eighties, it seems, reach their limit rather earlier than their pilots; in my day, it was generally the other way round.

Speed is a relative commodity. But it does not, I think, relate to fear - not unless you are trying to break the sound barrier on land or something of that sort. I don't believe that drivers need feel any more frightened going through Club corner flat out than I did negotiating Abbey without lifting. To *me* the idea of taking Club flat out is frightening, because it is not something I can conceive as being possible. On the other hand, I have never driven a modern Formula One car. I did have a go in Jackie Stewart's 1973 Tyrrell, but that was way before ground effect came in and it was only a half-hearted effort, around part of the Donington Park circuit. I remember being more impressed with the braking capabilities than the roadholding, but in any case I never got anywhere near the limit: the car was, frankly, vastly quicker round corners than I was used to and I had no intention of putting bravery before knowhow.

Courage has indeed always been a bigger factor in the racing driver's makeup than most of us would care to admit. Driving faster than the next man does take courage, no matter how much talent you've got. I used to frighten myself fairly regularly when I was racing - although usually I would feel frightened after the moment rather than while it was happening. The accident at Spa, when the wheel fell off, was not frightening at the time because I had to do everything I could to try and save my life; I just did not have the time to think about the real consequences while I was winding away at the wheel. At Monza, on the other hand, when the steering sheared on my Maserati, I had time to be frightened and I was, very. The accident happened at 165 mph, on the banking, and I have never felt so helpless. The steering had gone and the brakes were those of a 1,500cc sports car and therefore useless. Centrifugal force had taken control and I was convinced I was going over the top. I didn't, but the car took an awfully long time to stop and gave me plenty of time to convince myself that I had had it.

Accidents apart, there were many occasions when I would go through a corner faster than usual, straighten up and then think, 'Christ, I don't know how I managed to get away with that!' It was something that happened on quite a few occasions, because such is the nature of motor racing. That much, I'm sure, hasn't changed. What has changed, very much for the better, is the rate at which drivers are killed or injured. There is no doubt that modern safety precautions work exceedingly well. I am against putting driver safety before any other consideration but clearly certain measures, like fireproof clothing, roll-over bars and safety fuel cells, are highly desirable. I think Armco barrier has been something of a mixed blessing but I am all for catch fencing, where there is room to erect it. What I don't like to see is the spectators being pushed further and further away from the action merely for the benefit of the driver. Grand Prix racing is a spectator sport as much as football or tennis and I believe the enjoyment of those who go along to watch, paying heavily for the privilege, needs to be protected just as much as the well-being of the participants.

Reducing the risk of fire has probably been the greatest safety achievement, and that, of course, involves only the design of the car, not the circuit. Not since poor Roger Williamson was killed in 1973 has fire played a major role in any Formula One accident. When Ronnie Peterson's Lotus crashed at Monza in 1978 and exploded, everyone expected the worst - and sadly they were right. The sight of smoke and flame had become so rare that it was automatic to assume that Ronnie would perish in it. In fact, he was pulled clear by his fellow drivers and survived until next morning; by a cruel twist of fate it was not burns which killed Ronnie, but complications following an operation to set his broken bones.

I am indeed delighted to find that, despite the increased speed, modern Grand Prix drivers have less to fear than those of my era. Research carried out with motor racing journalist John Thompson shows that the incidence of fatal accidents has slowed dramatically. In the Formula One of 1954-60, twenty-six of the competing drivers died in accidents. Not all of them were killed behind the wheel of a Formula One car, but they were all Formula One drivers and my contemporaries. From 1961-70 there were twenty-four fatalities involving F1 drivers and from 1971-79 a further fourteen. You don't have to be a mathematical genius to determine that the rate of fatal accidents has fallen sharply since the fifties, and that the happy trend is continuing. Deaths amongst Formula Two drivers have become even more rare and I am delighted to find that sports car racing, at one time cursed with a morbid reputation for serious accidents, is now almost as safe as Kart racing.

But does this welcome reduction in fatalities prove that Grand Prix drivers have become more skilled? Or that their cars have become more solid? Amazingly, it would seem that there are even more accidents in Grand Prix racing now than there were in the 'dangerous' fifties. For, despite its inbuilt sophistication and notwithstanding the superb level of preparation now attained in F1, the modern Grand Prix car breaks with disturbing frequency. Wheels fall off (Didier Pironi lost *five* wheels during the 1979 season - unbelievable!), suspensions wilt, brakes fail and tyres explode. Sheer speed, it seems, does take its toll in terms of reliability and, in their desperate quest for maximum competitiveness, it may be that designers are leaving precious little margin for safety. It might have been the same in my day but, as I say, when a wishbone pulled out and the car went out of control it would be travelling at 90 mph where today's cars would be doing 140. At 90 you could still do something about it – stand on the brakes, spin the car, anything. At 140 you don't normally have very much time even to realise that you're in trouble so it's a case of off the track and thump into the barrier.

There's no doubt that technology offers an artificial kind of advantage which no amount of driving skill can duplicate. James Hunt discovered this and so, I think, did Niki Lauda. The problem is that whereas in my day the failings in a car *could* be compensated for behind the wheel, cars of the modern era are simply too sophisticated for the driver to make his skill and courage worth much. If, in the fifties and sixties, speed round a circuit was 50 per cent attributable to the car and 50 per cent to the driver, today it is something like 90 per cent car and only 10 per cent driver. For this reason, I would like to see all extraneous devices done away with; skirts and wings should go the way of the wide tyre.

Quite why there should be so much opposition to making changes of this kind I'm not sure. The tyre companies would obviously have to co-operate, but I'm certain that if rim widths were reduced, say, to nine or ten inches, with the extra proviso that every racing tyre should possess a minimum tread pattern, then better, closer, more spectacular motor racing should result, with greater spin-off, hopefully, for the ordinary motorist. It must make sense to the tyre firms to produce racing tyres which bear at least a passing resemblance to the ordinary road tyre. The contemporary 20-inch slicks have as much to do with the tyres on the family Cortina, or even the family Rolls Royce, as a bicycle wheel. If reducing their width would result in better racing, it surely follows that banning slicks would result in an improved 'public image'. Slick tyres are, in any event, a mixed blessing. They are useless, indeed highly dangerous, when it rains, as witness the scenes at several Grand Prix races over the past seven or eight years. Sixteen cars crashed at Silverstone during the 1975 British Grand Prix and it was those slick tyres, not the sudden downpour, that were to blame. I'm not suggesting that there should be one sort of tyre only, merely that *treadless* tyres should be outlawed. In this way a 'dry' tyre would still carry sufficient tread to cope with heavy rain at least to the point where the car could remain on the circuit. Wheel changes in the pits are part of the excitement and drama of racing and I'm all for that continuing. The sight of car after car slamming helplessly into the fencing merely because the weather suddenly turns sour is one that should not be repeated.

As far as wings and skirts are concerned, I would have thought that most people in racing would secretly prefer to see the back of them. Aerodynamics remains a black art in motor racing and I see more to be gained in concentrating on producing cars which are wind-cheating rather than wind-utilising. Producing low-drag designs which made the most of the available power would again benefit racing by improving straight-line speed while at the same time enjoying an advantage in terms of fuel economy. We all know that a smooth-bodied road car goes faster and uses less petrol than a bulky one. I see no reason why Grand Prix cars should not develop the theme and indeed break new ground.

If Grand Prix racing is to survive in the long term, I'm positive that some sort of fuel-effective formula will have to be introduced. There is nothing basically wrong, for example, in saying, 'Look, you can run whatever engine you like but you mustn't use more than twenty gallons of fuel. If you do, you must make a pit-stop.' I'm in favour of pit-stops because I believe they add excitement and interest. The most expensive seats are always facing or above the pits and the people who pay to watch from there should be given value for money.

If constrictions *were* made relative to the use of fuel, and the size and type of tyre, few other rules need apply. Ideally, designers could be left completely free as far as power units were concerned. Certain regulations controlling minimum weight and maximum size would be required, and, as I say, I feel that 'artificial' aerodynamic aids should be banned. A formula of this nature would be very interesting technically – one might see a return to four-wheel-drive, for instance, something of which I'm all in favour. It might, of course, prove overburdeningly expensive, but I'm trying here to lay down what would make for improved *racing*, not what would necessarily offer the best return on an investment.

In my experience the more rules you have in motor racing, the worse things seem to become. Indianapolis-style racing in the United States has always seemed to have fewer constraints than Formula One racing and, while technically the Americans have lagged behind the Europeans, the racing itself has flourished. The drivers seem by and large to have a far more ebullient approach to racing than their Grand Prix counterparts. Despite the very high speeds which 'Indy' cars attain (today the engines are mostly turbocharged 3-litre Cosworth-Ford DFV, renamed the DFX, running on alcohol and developing over 700 bhp), the prospect of injury or worse appears to deter the Indy drivers not at all – they simply go on and on. If you're not at least forty years old you're still considered a youngster! These guys are all 'real racers', tough as they come but phlegmatic with it. It would be nice if more Grand Prix drivers had the same attitude.

Indianapolis cars run on narrower tyres than F1 (14 inches I believe) and ground effect technology is only just rearing its head. When John Webb brought over a gridful of such machinery to Britain in 1978, we witnessed a fascinating alternative to Grand Prix racing, one which I personally think has more potential. The drivers were largely unaccustomed to European-style circuits and for some of them racing at Silverstone and Brands Hatch was a very strange experience indeed – certainly nothing like the oval racing they were used to. But they broke the outright lap record at both tracks and the sight of men like Danny Ongais, A. J. Foyt, Al Unser and Rick Mears wrestling with wheelspin right round the circuit was a highly impressive one. As an indication of the difference in performance between an Indy car and an F1 car, consider the top speed recorded for Ongais in his Parnelli-Cosworth DFX at Brands Hatch. For various reasons the organisers chose to run the car on the 'club' circuit of 1.2 miles instead of the Grand Prix course of 2.61 miles. This meant that the top straight was preceded by the very slow right-hander at Clearways instead of the much faster corner used with the full circuit. Grand Prix cars take this faster corner at well over 100 mph and peak along the top straight at around 165 before braking for Paddock Bend. Ongais, despite coming on to the straight some thirty miles an hour slower than the Grand Prix cars, was timed at 172 mph before Paddock, ample proof of the fabulous acceleration of the turbocharged machine and an indication, too, of how hard Ongais had to lean on the brake pedal to slow down for the next corner. I'm not suggesting that Grand Prix racing should switch overnight to Indianapolis-type rules, but for my money the Indy cars are nearer to the ideal than the current Formula One.

I would also like to imagine that changes in Grand Prix design would lead to a return to natural-looking circuits. It's significant, surely, that those courses which used to be regarded as absolute classics in my day have practically all disappeared, unable to keep pace with the type of road surface the modern car needs and the safety precautions subsequently demanded. Spa in its original form has gone and so have Reims, Rouen, Bremgarten, Solitude, Pescara and, saddest of all, the mighty Nurburgring. In some cases, notably at Spa, I can see that the cost of installing sufficient safety precautions to protect the spectators must indeed have proved outrageously high. In other instances, as in the case of the Nurburgring, it is 'driver power' which has hastened their end - where demands for the 'ultimate safety' of those taking part have proved impractical. Some circuits have bowed to the will of the drivers and installed extensive, and expensive, modifications - Monte Carlo is one, Zandvoort another. But all the time the spectators get a rougher deal while paying more money. It would be better by far to alter the cars to suit existing tracks rather than the tracks to suit the cars. The trend towards what I regarded as ill-advised alterations started while I was still racing, and I spoke out against them at the time. I remember back in 1959 being interviewed at Sebring during practice for what was the first Grand Prix of the USA. Sebring was, and still is, an airfield circuit, about as featureless as you can imagine. Its one saving grace in those days was a section comprising genuine roads which supplemented the never-ending runways. The FIA (Fédération Internationale de l'Automobile) were creating a hoo-ha over this and in a recorded interview with an American reporter I said:

'As a circuit, I feel that Sebring would be better with a few brick walls and trees and houses round it. I think this is a general feeling amongst Grand Prix drivers - I know it is amongst Tony Brooks and Cliff Allison and myself because we were discussing it last night. We feel that Sebring lacks character because it is an aerodrome, and we feel that once we get on to the "road" section things are a lot better.

'It's amazing, but the FIA were trying to stop the organisers from using the road section at all. This just shows the state into which the governing body of motor racing has degraded the sport. They are gradually doing their best to ruin our sport, and I hope that America will join with England and Italy in doing what we can to stop it. Sebring isn't the best of circuits and it isn't the worst, but without that road section I believe it would be the worst, at least for a Grand Prix.

'I noticed, too, that the organisers have cut down a lot of trees in the Esses. This I was sorry to see. Let's face it, this race is a World Championship event and I think everybody feels it should be run on a proper road circuit. Therefore, the nearer we can keep this to looking like a road, the better. Roads signify to us trees and telegraph poles, ditches and banks, houses and kerbstones. We haven't got any of those around here.'

This was over twenty years ago but my general view remains the same. Road racing as I knew it has disappeared and I would love to see it return. I suppose it's up to the constructors to admit to each other that things have gone too far and for the FIA through its sporting division FISA (Fédération Internationale Sportive Automobile) – formerly the CSI (Commission Sportive Internationale) – to cease being negative and ineffectual. The time has come for them actually to do something which would be of genuine benefit to the sport as a whole and not just to one or two interested parties. Frankly, I don't think there's much chance that this will happen.

MIKE HAILWOOD

I'm not cut out to be a prophet of doom, but I do believe that if major changes don't take place soon in Grand Prix racing there will be a great big accident that could stop it all. As things stand today we have exotically designed vehicles hammering faster and faster round circuits less and less able to contain them. Overtaking is ridiculously difficult and therefore ridiculously dangerous. The performance of the machines really lies in the hands of the designers, not the drivers, with the result that the guy behind the wheel is no longer master of his own destiny.

It's frustrating for drivers and for spectators. Who wants to watch a high speed parade of cars following each other round and round, waiting for mechanical failure to eliminate them one by one? How can a driver hope to test and improve his skills?

I'm afraid that it will take the inevitable shunt, with a car somersaulting at very high speed into the crowd killing 20 or 30 people to bring home the point. And if it does happen, then we might well have to kiss goodbye to motor racing altogether. It was touch-and-go back in 1955 when Levegh's Mercedes ploughed into the crowd at Le Mans. There was a big move then to ban all racing and to this day circuit racing is forbidden in Switzerland.

Lessons were learned from that tragedy and safety precautions quite rightly improved. But now time has caught up again, and I think that things are getting out of control. Feelings are already running very high in Germany and Sweden, and I'm sure that another calamity on the scale of Le Mans - and it won't need to be as bad as that - would give the anti-motorsport lobby all the ammunition it needs to force a total clampdown.

Even in my later days we were rushing along fairly briskly. But in '73 and '74 we were positively snail-like in the corners in comparison with today's cars. It is cornering speed, achieved through ground effect technology and ever-wider and stickier tyres, which has gone through the roof.

Back in 1973, before they put in the chicane at Woodcote, Ronnie Peterson put his Lotus 72 on pole position at Silverstone in a time of 1 minute 16.3 seconds, or 138.1 mph. This was reckoned to be pretty quick at the time and I know I thought it was fast because I could only manage 1 minute 18 seconds with the old Surtees!

In 1975, the first year the chicane was used, pole time for the Grand Prix dropped to a 'mere' 1 minute 19.36 seconds or 133.0 mph, set by Tom Pryce. In practice for the 1979 Grand Prix, Alan Jones lapped at a staggering six-and-a-half seconds inside the official lap record (held by Danny Ongais in his USAC Parnelli-Cosworth DFX) to take pole position. His time was

1 minute 11.8 seconds – 146.84 mph! Jonesy was able to make mincemeat of any and every previous lap time at Silverstone in spite of the chicane. For years in Grand Prix racing we have been used to lap records being beaten by fifths, tenths and hundredths of a second. For Alan in the Williams to be so devastatingly fast, to be so much quicker than anyone else before, was almost unbelievable. His effort constituted the finest hour for the ground effect theory that year, and it underlined the enormous improvement made since my day.

Enormous improvement? To me it seems more like a crazy improvement! Here's Jonesy and the rest making the heroes of yesteryear look as if they weren't trying. This gigantic 'advance' in technology, the introduction of ground effect (combined with tyre development), has produced this enormous leap forward in speed through the turns, and I'm surprised that the drivers' brains can keep up with it! I honestly get the feeling that many of them are living on borrowed time. Going through corners so much faster means that an accident, when it happens, is going to be that much bigger and proportionately nastier.

I agree with Stirling when he calls for the banning of ground effect aerodynamics and the reduction of rim widths from 20 inches to nine or ten. The onus of making a racing car go fast round a circuit should surely return to the driver. It's only fair to put him back 'in charge' because right now it seems patently obvious to me that the car does almost the whole job. These may sound like drastic measures, but I think drastic measures are needed. I'm all in favour of Formula One cars rushing as fast as they can down the straights but I think they must be slowed down in corners. And while we're on the subject of rushing down straights, I would just like to add that I am *not* in favour of turbocharged engines!

Although all the cars these days look super quick, I get the impression that they are not all that difficult to drive. Formula Three drivers today make what used to be regarded as the giant step to Formula One and become stars almost overnight. In the old days drivers were around for a long time learning and honing their skills before they became 'stars'. I'm sure that a lot of the genuine aces must be frustrated by the limitations placed on their abilities by these cars. They just do not appear to

Moss winning his first Championship Grand Prix in 1955 at Aintree driving the Mercedes-Benz W196. (*Photo:* LAT Photographic)

Hailwood swings the Honda through the gooseneck on his way to victory in the 1967 250cc TT. (*Photo:* B. R. Nicholls)

This dramatic Nurburgring sequence shows how Mike Hailwood's four-wheel career ended. *Opposite:* his McLaren M23 veers sharp right after landing awkwardly at the Pflanzgarten jump. *Above:* the car spinning wildly down the road, its front end already smashed as Ronnie Peterson in the Lotus 76 goes through. The McLaren eventually came to rest sixty yards from the initial point of impact *(below)*. *Overleaf:* rescuers took some time to cut Hailwood free. (*Photos:* von Rüden)

Above: Pictures from Stirling Moss' personal scrap book showing his crash at Goodwood on Easter Monday 1962.

Above: Hailwood on his way to victory in the 1979 Senior TT on the Isle of Man.

Below: Early success: Twenty-one-year-old Hailwood on the 500 Norton winning his first Senior TT on the Isle of Man. (*Photo:* B. R. Nicholls)

Above: Past and present: Hailwood, ten times world motorcycle champion, with Barry Sheene, 500cc champion in 1976 and 1977. (*Photo:* B. R. Nicholls)

Mike Hailwood astride the 500cc MV-Agusta 4 in the 1965 Senior TT at Quarter Bridge which he won. (*Photo:* B. R. Nicholls)

Above: Moss behind the wheel of Jackie Stewart's 1973 championship-winning Tyrrell-Ford at Donington Park – the first and indeed only time he sampled a 'modern' Grand Prix single-seater. (*Photo:* London Art Tech.)

Below: Stirling Moss leading the 1954 Italian Grand Prix in his 'own' Formula One 250F Maserati. (*Photo:* LAT Photographic)

ght: Moss slides
ınd the La Source
ırpin at
a-Francorchamps
a works-entered
)F Maserati to
ke third place in
1956 Belgian
and Prix.
ıoto: LAT
otographic)

low: **Moss, with side panels cut away on his Rob Walker Lotus 18, leads Richie nther's Ferrari and Joachim** Bonnier's Porsche in the 1961 Monaco Grand Prix. *hoto:* LAT Photographic)

Today's bulletin says: A slight but definite improvement

ATKINSON MORLEY'S HOSPITAL

MOSS: 'LIFE NOT IN DANGER'—FATHER

What went wrong?

By ROBERT WALLING

Did Moss's new V-8 engine in his Lotus cut dead on St. Mary's bend, so causing his crash.

Today I learned RAC scrutineers, who carefully examined it last night, found the engine's distributor cap was uncoupled, which would have denied current to the sparking plugs.

But the big point still undecided was this: did the cap jump loose as Stirling began going through the bend at 140 m.p.h., or did the crash itself cause the damage?

But what the preliminary examination did show was:

BRAKES were in good order;

THROTTLE LINKAGE, with which Moss had trouble earlier in the 100 miles race, was in fair shape.

STEERING, though badly damaged, appeared to be in order.

So the distributor cap has been removed for further examination to determine whether it had anything to do with the crash.

Crumpled wreckage

The crumpled wreckage of the car came by lorry after the scrutineers' look at it to the Highgate headquarters of the U.D.T.-Laystall racing team. It will be examined again and a further report made later this week.

"Nobody outside the racing team will be allowed to see it. Racing drivers hate to have a crashed car put on view after the event," said a U.D.T. official today.

But the question "What caused it?" was being discussed among Moss's racing driver friends.

"If it was not brakes, not steering, and the distributor was damaged by the impact—then what?" they asked.

Moss did not get to the peak of the car racing world, earning at least £50,000 a year, by charging out of control through a bend on a track where not even an official Grand Prix race is held.

Did he 'lose it'?

All the same Moss is human. He has crashed before. At Aintree I have seen him spin at more than 100 m.p.h. on a wet surface and with terrific dexterity carry on in the right direction with hardly any loss of speed.

Did he "lose it"—That is, [illegible] too fast through St. Mary's [illegible] what he just [illegible]?

HIS FATHER: Mr. Alfred Moss stands beside the stretcher as Stirling, a dressing on his injured head, is carried from the ambulance at the hospital in Wimbledon today.

He is still unconscious —no operation at present

Evening Standard Reporter

Alfred Moss left the London bedside of his son Stirling for a few moments today and said: "My son's life is not in danger. There was never any suggestion that it was."

Mr. Moss, anxious but confident of his son's recovery, had spent some 20 hours near his boy since the 110 m.p.h. horror crash at Goodwood yesterday.

"It will take a little time," he explained. "A brain injury is always serious, therefore they are taking this very great care of him."

As Mr. Moss stood outside the pale-pink Brodie Ward at the Atkinson Morley Hospital in Wimbledon he also spoke of the "not to worry" message which Stirling's mother got yesterday afternoon.

"I sent it," said Mr. Moss. "Stirling was unconscious after the crash and has remained so."

Today's first news about Stirling's condition came in a hospital bulletin issued by the secretary, Mr. Laurence Brown. It said:

"Now there is no doubt that Mr. Stirling Moss has sustained quite a severe head injury with additional damage to the left shoulder and left knee joint, as well as a fractured rib. His condition since admission has shown slight but definite improvemtn although he has not yet regained consciousness. There is no question of an operation at the present time."

A further bulletin will be issued this evening.

The 32-year-old British ace was examined this morning by Mr. Wylie McKissock, one of the world's leading brain specialists.

Senior consultant surgeon at the hospital, Mr. McKissock, arrived at nine o'clock.

Afterwards the hospital secretary said that Moss was still seriously ill, despite the slight improvement. But he stressed that the surgeon had decided that it would not be necessary to operate immediately.

Stirling may later be moved to a private ward.

He was transferred to the Atkinson Morley at 1.45 this morning from the Royal West Sussex Hospital, Chichester.

With him went his father.

Mr. Ken Gregory, Stirling's manager, also spent several hours at the hospital. He drove back to his Kingston home just before dawn. Later he returned and spoke to Stirling's father and the surgeons.

[illegible] said.

"I'm going to my home [illegible] Tring, Hertfordshire, first of [illegible]. Everything is so very confu[sed] and I'm not sure what I sh[all] be doing exactly."

HIS SECRETARY: Miss Vale[rie] Pirie arrives at the Royal W[est] Sussex Hospital to see Stirl[ing] before he was taken [to] Wimbledon.

THE SURGEON: Mr. Wylie McKissock, one of the world's leading brain specialists.

HIS MANAGER: Ken Gregory at the Atkinson Morley Hospital today. He spent several hours there during the night.

STIRLING MOSS'S CRASH BAFFLES EXPERTS

Above: Newspaper cuttings from the time of Stirling Moss' near-fatal crash at Goodwood.

Opposite: Stirling Moss in his heyday, with Graham Hill behind. (*Photo:* Geoffrey Goddard)

DUNLOP

Above: Juan Manuel Fangio – in Moss' view the greatest Grand Prix driver of all time – at Aintree in 1957 in the 250F 2.5 litre Maserati. (*Photo:* Geoffrey Goddard)

Below: Grand Prix cars of yesteryear were small enough to race two and three abreast. This is Monza in 1963, Graham Hill leading from John Surtees. Mike Hailwood finished tenth in this race. (*Photo:* Keystone)

Derek Minter was the hardest rider Hailwood ever faced. Here Minter powers to victory in the 1962 250cc TT on the Honda-4. (*Photo:* B. R. Nicholls)

The way they were. Stirling in the Vanwall graphically illustrates the full-blooded four wheel drift at Silverstone in 1958.

Moss in the Lotus-Climax 18/21 V8 leads John Surtees (Lola-Climax Mk. 4) in the 1962 Brussels Grand Prix. Moss' crash at Goodwood was in this car.

Pure road circuits have all but disappeared in modern motor racing. This shot shows Willy Mairesse (Ferrari) leading the field in the 1962 Brussels Grand Prix.

The modern racer: Gilles Villeneuve in the wide-bodied, wide-tyred Ferrari 312T5. Two such cars side by side fill the width of the contemporary race track. (*Photo:* LAT Photographic)

Four world champions – Jackie Stewart, Juan Fangio, Denny Hulme and John Surtees – play a supporting role to Stirling during the Pace Petroleum Moss Day at Brands Hatch, summer 1980. (*Photo:* LAT Photographic)

The new Moss behind the wheel of the 1.6 litre Akai Audi 80 at Mallory Park. (*Photo:* LAT Photographic)

respond to extra-brilliant drivers like Hunt, Lauda, Reutemann and Andretti. I know I used to get frustrated in the seventies because of my limitations when it came to setting up cars, but at least the driver still counted. If you were really 'on song' one day, you most definitely *could* beat the field. Just look at the way Hunt beat Lauda in Holland in '75 to win his first-ever Grand Prix - that was really a *driver's* victory.

I'm all for giving the spectators more for their money, so I'd really like to see something done to reintroduce those thrilling overtaking manoeuvres we used to see. I'd like to see the cars made narrower and tyre widths reduced too. This would make them easier to overtake and much more exciting to watch. I'd like to see the drivers more instantly recognisable as well. At the moment they sit buried in their cars and they could be anybody. The spectators can't see what's going on in the cockpit. The drivers don't move the wheel very much any more, and if the racing looks dull *to me,* then I hate to think what the spectator makes of it!

Of course, no matter what changes are brought in, no-one can turn the clock back to the days of the Nurburgring, Spa, Rouen and Reims. Those circuits, at least in the form I knew them, have gone for good. However, drivers have become too used to *not* competing on road circuits and the sport depends too much today on massive safety precautions, catch fencing and Armco barrier. Mind you I'm not about to knock Armco barrier. I have every reason to be thankful that I hit Armco - and German Armco at that - when I crashed at the Ring in 1974.

Drivers are entitled to be safety conscious - it's their lives on the line after all. This huge safety business has become such an important factor in the sport now that no-one can expect drivers to make an about-turn and agree to the suitability of the 'old-style' circuits, no matter what changes are made to the cars.

But changes will have to be made, because you can't keep on messing about with circuits year after year in a desperate attempt to cope with speeds which are becoming crazier and crazier. When was the last great purge on the circuit owners? The early seventies? They were forced to spend millions of pounds on bringing tracks up to date on the understanding that they would thereafter be considered 'safe'. Take the Nurburgring, for example. The organisers had to shift the 1970 German Grand Prix from the Ring, its traditional home, to Hockenheim. One could hardly imagine two more different circuits. The Ring has 14 miles of twisting, turning road, swooping up, down and around the Eifel forests. It's impossible to learn thoroughly, every lap presents a different challenge. Hockenheim, on the other hand, runs for just over four miles - still a respectable length by modern standards - and it is almost totally featureless. There's virtually no hope of overtaking and for the benefit of the spectators, who are all gathered together in the huge concrete grandstands of the 'stadium', there's a twiddly, mickey-mouse section just before the start-finish line, where all you can try to do is not to spin off! I've never raced there in Formula One, only in Formula 5000 and Formula Two, but it was never one of my favourite venues.

In 1971 the Grand Prix returned to the Nurburgring. The organisers had removed acres of forest, blasted away rock faces, installed miles and miles of guard rails and catch fencing and everyone was satisfied that the Ring was once more the ideal place to run a Grand Prix. But in 1977 the race was transferred to Hockenheim, where it has been ever since, because the Ring was decreed too dangerous for Formula One. Isn't it about time people started looking at the cars which are making these circuits too dangerous?

Personally, I never thought the Nurburgring was any less safe than anywhere else, but I can see that to cope with ground effect cars it would have to be further modified. So it's more convenient to race at Hockenheim. As John Watson said, 'I'd much rather race at the Ring, but I'd rather survive at Hockenheim'. The tragedy is that in the name of safety, modern circuits are built in such a way as to lack any of the character of the older traditional ones. Sure, some of the older circuits have survived, but they are forced to make more and more changes every year so as to keep pace, safety-wise, with lap times. For the driver, challenges, like the Ring and Spa, no longer exist.

There could be other changes to Grand Prix racing too that would put a bit more fire in its belly. As a gesture to the energy crisis some kind of methanol-based fuel will eventually have to be used. Methanol burns faster than petrol so I'm not sure how much 'energy' would actually be conserved by using it, but since the amount of fuel used in an entire Grand Prix season is no more than that burnt up by a Boeing Jumbo jet flying once across the Atlantic and back, the whole argument is wobbly, to say the least! Still there could be some kind of ruling which would make it seem that Grand Prix racing was doing its bit in the search for greater economy and I think Stirling has a good point when he calls for a limit on the amount of fuel a Grand Prix car should carry.

By saying that I certainly don't mean that I should like to see the races themselves shortened - in fact, quite the opposite! I would like to see them get quite a bit longer. What is it nowadays at Monza? One and a quarter hours or so? Spectators are paying out a fortune to see cars go round and round for less time than it takes to play a football match (not that I've ever been to a football match!). You could argue that people would get bored with longer contests. With racing being one long procession as it seems to be today, I agree. In fact they might become bored within five minutes!

Let's bring the spectacle back - then the audience would be begging for longer races. We used to race for over two hours in a Grand Prix in the sixties, why not today? Drivers today certainly aren't any less fit than we were then - in fact, they are probably much fitter! And if there had to be a pit-stop to take on more fuel, all well and good. It would all add to the excitement and the spectacle.

I don't honestly think anyone would really suffer if cornering was radically limited. Sure, designers would be snookered by the rules initially, but they'd soon think of other things to compensate. It would save the circuits a fortune and it would save the constructors a fortune. And the closer racing would attract more spectators, more TV coverage and more sponsors. The drivers would really be able to exhibit *their* skills and the World Championship would have greater meaning.

It seems to me that many of the top men in motor racing have become blinded to the threat of a major disaster. We've had warning signs in Barcelona and in Japan and anyone who has been around racing for any length of time knows what happens when a car goes out of control in a corner. Some circuits could cope, but others would be found sadly wanting.

Can we afford to take the risk? I don't think so. Motor racing is and always has been a dangerous sport. What is the point of making it any more dangerous than it need be at the expense of the skills which it once nurtured? Let's do something now, before that tragedy occurs and it's too late to be sorry.

5 Driver power

STIRLING MOSS

I would like to see drivers commanding not so much 'power' in motor sport but 'influence', although I appreciate it's sometimes difficult to distinguish between the two. Certainly I've always believed that the men behind the wheel, those with the most to lose as well as the most to gain out of racing, should have a solid say in the way their sport is run. A driver's viewpoint surely has just as much right to be heard as those of the constructors or the organisers. However, how to unify those views and bring them sensibly to bear has always posed something of a problem.

Central control of Grand Prix racing, by which I mean control by the FIA (Fédération Internationale de l'Automobile) from Paris, has for years been weak and questionable. The traditional inability of the FIA's sporting arm (FISA) to make the right decisions has made it all the more important for individual factions to speak with a powerful voice. In 1980 FISA, via its president Jean-Marie Balestre, tended to call the shots, but it's the constructors through FOCA (Formula One Constructors' Association) who speak the most positively. The organisers, while having to bow to the demands of FOCA, generally do quite nicely out of running a Grand Prix (which is why Bernie Ecclestone himself now organises several rounds of the World Championship!), but I'm afraid that the drivers, and their opinions, are all too often ignored. Admittedly, over the years, there have been few occasions when they have acted in a uniform manner, and even when they succeeded in doing so, their line of argument has often led to controversy.

The last major stand by the drivers occurred back in 1975, at the Spanish Grand Prix in Barcelona. The events of that race brought a sourness to the sport which had not been previously suspected. Acrimony was created where previously there had been friendship, contracts were broken and confusion reigned. The problem lay in the circuit. Situated in the beautiful Montjuich Park on the hillside overlooking the town, it was an old-style Grand Prix venue, full of interest and winding through a natural setting. Every time there was a race the public roads would be converted into a race track at the last possible moment. However by 1975 Armco barrier was considered a necessity – quite rightly, if only to protect the spectators – and this had to be erected during the day or two before practice was due to start. In the year in question, the teams arrived to find the barriers in a terrible state; bolts were missing and in some cases whole sections could be pushed over by hand. Naturally enough, the drivers complained, the majority refusing to practise until the barriers had been properly screwed together.

At this point, unhappily, all the various parties involved retreated into their shells. A constitutional crisis set in with the organisers, the constructors, the drivers and representatives of the governing body all reprimanding each other. The first day's practice was completely lost and, despite overnight repairs, the drivers, led by the then World Champion, Emerson Fittipaldi, remained adamant that the barriers were still not secure enough. The matter was apparently deadlocked until someone remembered that if the cars did not race, the sum due to be paid out in prize money to the constructors would have to be paid in reverse. The teams, in other words, would have had to pay a huge penalty to the organisers, and the thought of having to fork out tens of thousands (the cars would have been impounded until the money was forthcoming) brought extra pressure to bear on the drivers, some of whom I believe were threatened with the sack.

Eventually they did reluctantly practise but as the grid formed up for the race itself Fittipaldi was missing; he had packed his bags and gone. Emerson obviously believed very strongly that the track was still unsafe and maybe he was right. After twenty-four laps Rolf Stommelen's car shed its rear wing and crashed, taking the lives of five onlookers and injuring ten more. However, the car had actually flown *over* the Armco, not through it, and in other accidents the barrier was seen to do its job well. The race was stopped, of course, and Grand Prix cars have not competed at Montjuich since. Afterwards, the motoring press handed out quite a pasting to the drivers, and particularly to poor Fittipaldi who at least had demonstrated the courage of his convictions. But whichever point of view one takes, the clear fact of the fiasco was that the drivers lost their battle and that the constructors and the organisers won. Once the issue of money became of greater significance than that of safety, the result was never in doubt.

The standing of the Grand Prix Drivers' Association suffered thereafter, which was particularly disappointing to me because I had actually helped start the association back in 1957. After Barcelona it was effectively disbanded until 1980 when Jody Scheckter announced his intention to re-form it. Whether Jody can do a good job of unifying his colleagues *and* influencing the form and style of Grand Prix racing remains to be seen - I wish him luck. But to put matters into perspective I ought to explain that my reasons for founding an alliance of drivers had little to do with the current obsession with safety. It was not our aim to make the sport very much safer, except where the public was concerned, nor did we involve ourselves as a group in finance; drivers did their deals individually. The idea was to band together so as to make concerted suggestions for the improvement and betterment of racing. We wanted to make the sport more successful and more attractive. We certainly did not intend to issue threats, or indulge in militancy.

Ironically, the first mistake we made was to give the association a French title (French being the official language of racing) which confused some people into thinking that we were all about to go on strike! The name we chose was the Union des Pilotes Professionales Internationales, which was abbreviated to UPPI, but the use of the word 'union' was like a red rag to a bull as far as certain members of the national press were concerned. One British daily paper came out with the headline, 'Racing Drivers Start Union' and went on to talk about the 'discontent' of Europe's Grand Prix drivers. The main suspicion at the time was that we were out to force organisers to pay higher starting money. Nothing could have been further from the truth.

The obvious way round the misunderstanding was to rename

our 'union' and by 1961, therefore, it had become the Grand Prix Drivers' Association (GPDA). The inaugural meeting was held at the Hotel Metropole in Monte Carlo on 11 May 1961. Racing journalist Peter Garnier was appointed secretary of the association and in his book about the Monaco Grand Prix, *Sixteen on the Grid,* he spells out the original aims. He has kindly given me permission to reproduce that first press bulletin here. It read:

Monte Carlo, 6 pm, 11 May 1961
'International racing drivers have today formed themselves into a new group, to be called the Grand Prix Drivers' Association. Founder members are as follows:

Cliff Allison	Olivier Gendebien	Stirling Moss
Joachim Bonnier	Dan Gurney	Henry Taylor
Jack Brabham	Graham Hill	Maurice Trintignant
Tony Brooks	Innes Ireland	Wolfgang von Trips
Jimmy Clark	Bruce McLaren	Roy Salvadori
Masten Gregory	Phil Hill	John Surtees

'The aims of the Association are:
1 To obtain international recognition, and to seek to obtain representation on the Commission Sportive Internationale (CSI), the governing body of international motor sport.
2 To further the aims of motor racing by co-operating with national and international bodies already in existence.
3 To co-operate in bringing about improvements in the safety provisions for both spectators and drivers.
4 Membership will be by invitation; qualifications will be active participation in Grand Prix racing.

'Stirling Moss and Joachim Bonnier were unanimously elected Chairman and Vice-Chairman respectively; and Peter Garnier was elected Honorary Member to take on the duties of Honorary Secretary and Honorary Treasurer.

'*Footnote:* This means that there is now in existence an Association of Grand Prix drivers whose advice can be sought, and to which approaches can be made. Hitherto there has been no such international and fully representative body. Members intend to meet on the occasion of each World Championship race.'

Many of those original aims were achieved, including representation at meetings of the CSI. We also achieved improvements in flag marshalling and we persuaded the CSI to bring in their 'catch tank' rule which enabled oil from breathers to be collected on board the car rather than deposited on the road. We made several suggestions as to how circuits could be improved and I like to think the ideas put forward were of a positive, beneficial nature. Safety was obviously a topic for discussion but it was, as I say, the paying public about whom we were most concerned. The main difficulty we had, perhaps, was in persuading the drivers to actually turn up at meetings and to be constructive in their thinking. It was hard, really, to get them all to knuckle down and take the thing seriously. Some did, others tended not to bother. All racing drivers are complete individualists and there will always be some who fight shy of belonging to any organised group. Jacky Ickx, for instance, resigned from the GPDA; it wasn't that Jacky didn't care about the sport, he simply held different views to most drivers. As a Belgian he felt passionately about the great road course of Spa-Francorchamps and once the majority of drivers had refused to race Grand Prix cars there (the last time was in 1970) he actively shunned the GPDA's point of view on virtually everything. Jacky's love affair with Spa was finally fulfilled. After retiring from racing in 1979 he took over as director of the new, modified circuit.

In my day, however, I don't recall any top driver openly disagreeing with the Association, but there were certainly a few who left all the decision-making to others. This was probably one reason why, in the old days, the GPDA never had quite as much influence as I would have liked.

I am not in favour of drivers as a group boycotting a particular race or circuit. Indeed I have never been a supporter of negative attitudes whether in racing or anywhere else. If an individual driver feels strongly enough about a particular track I concede that it is his prerogative not to turn out. But it does surprise me that, in a sport which demands total commitment to the cause, such a prerogative is ever exercised.

In 1957 the UPPI denounced the running of a 500-mile race over the banked circuit at Monza in which Indianapolis machinery was pitched against European-style cars. We felt that such an event would be pointless since there was no Grand Prix car suitable to race against the American ones – not on the banked oval which was as inappropriate to F1 cars as it was ideal for the Indy vehicles. None of the top Grand Prix drivers competed and of course we were accused of being frightened off. In fact, in spite of our very real objections, the principal reason for our absence was the total lack of suitable cars. Naturally enough the Americans cleaned up, with only a handful of sports racing Jaguars as opposition.

The following year the race was staged again and this time an attempt was made to produce a few 'specials' loosely based on Grand Prix machinery. I felt no happier about competing than I had twelve months earlier, but this time there *was* a car for me to drive – a single-seater Maserati powered by a 4.2-litre sports car engine. Ferrari had also been persuaded to enter a team, but the basic problem remained: our cars simply weren't designed to take the constant hammering and g-forces associated with the harsh Monza banking. Even so, I was prepared to have a go because here was a new challenge. Backing down because I felt I might lose did not appeal to me.

In the race the steering sheared at 160 mph and I was lucky to escape unscathed. The breakage tended to justify my misgivings, and those of the UPPI the year before, but we Europeans – including Mike Hawthorn, Luigi Musso, Maurice Trintignant and Harry Schell – went on with it anyway. Boycotting the event would have let a lot of people down and would have done nothing to improve the stock of international motor sport.

Drivers today have just as much right as I did to complain about aspects of racing which displease them. I'd like to hear more from all of them, not just the odd one or two. But instead of demanding one more safety measure after another, I would prefer to see them attacking the root cause of the problem, cornering speed. The design of the cars needs more careful examination than that of the circuits and if the GPDA could, under the leadership of Jody Scheckter, help bring about a change in single-seater specification, then they would indeed gain a famous and worthwhile victory.

MIKE HAILWOOD

Persuading racing drivers to join together and speak with one voice is a bit like trying to unify parliament. What one driver thinks is a good idea, another will laugh at.

There's also a curious reluctance to take drivers' ideas seriously. Rightly or wrongly there have, over the years, been several instances when drivers have threatened to take the law into their own hands, but almost every time they have been denounced by the press and others as 'trouble makers'.

The point so many people miss when they criticise drivers for speaking out against certain aspects of the sport is that it is *their* lives and *their* livelihoods which are at stake. Racing drivers are professionals in a business which carries very high risks. It seems to me they have more right than most to voice their opinions, to air their doubts, and to state their fears.

Not that all drivers are necessarily worthy of acting as spokesmen for the sport. Sometimes those who moan the most about safety, or the lack of it, are themselves complete rockapes on the circuits! Take Riccardo Patrese's one-race ban at the end of 1978. That came in the aftermath of the Monza disaster in which Ronnie Peterson was killed, but for which Patrese was *not*, after all, responsible. He had doubtless been guilty of some over-enthusiastic driving on earlier occasions, but film of the Monza crash showed that he was not to blame. However, a lot of drivers who should have known better immediately decided otherwise and in an outburst of emotion they had Patrese banned. It was a 'kangaroo court' decision which didn't reflect too well on the intellect of Riccardo's so-called colleagues.

But lo and behold, look what happens in the first race of 1979. Two 'senior' drivers, among the most respected in the business, collide at the first corner causing the race to be stopped! Talk about those who live in glass houses. . . .

If you ban one driver, perhaps you should ban the lot, because everyone makes mistakes and has accidents from time to time. But whether what Stirling calls the 'ethics of racing' have worsened over recent years is another matter. There was a much-publicised incident in one Grand Prix in 1979 which made me wonder whether certain drivers have abandoned their instinct for self-preservation in mad bids for glory. The barging match to which I refer made good television, but it horrified me. If I could have had my way I would have banned the two men concerned not just for one race, but for the rest of the season.

The danger involved with motorsport is an emotive issue, of course, and it's all too easy to become paranoid about it. At the end of the sixties the big demand was for Armco barrier, until it was found that Armco was not, after all, the greatest thing since sliced bread. It probably saved my life, but in other instances it caused more damage than it avoided. Catch fencing is obviously a better idea but ironically it was the circuits themselves, rather than the drivers, who were responsible for its introduction.

What drivers need to do today is not, as is traditional, demand continued alterations to circuits, but to start working on their own bosses – the car constructors – in an attempt to alter the rules. In 1979, Jody Scheckter took up the cudgels to revive the Grand Prix Drivers' Association and insisted on a string of new chicanes. As a short-term method of reducing cornering speeds chicanes might be the answer – although there were certain instances, notably at Zandvoort, where many felt the new 'Jody chicane' offered a more dangerous hazard than the flat out curve it replaced! Jody doubtless thought he did a good job, but I know that other drivers viewed his efforts with suspicion. Perhaps they should have given him more support, because all the time they squabble amongst themselves they can hardly be expected to command proper respect.

Apart from the constructors themselves, almost everyone agrees that cornering ability must be diminished. The drivers have a golden opportunity to bring pressure to bear, and I'm pleased to say there are signs that their influence is finally having some effect. But again there's a rift of opinion. Some want side skirts to be banned; others, perhaps themselves influenced by the wishes of their team owners, have said that skirts should stay. Until they can all get round a table and work out a common policy it will still be the designers who rule.

I'm all for the GPDA bringing as much pressure to bear as it can. When I was racing cars the association was alive but not all that well, as I recall. Things were OK while Jackie Stewart was in charge and he achieved a lot on the safety front. But after Jackie retired at the end of 1973 things rather fell to pieces. I sincerely hope that Jody can successfully marshal his troops, but I have to say that he'll do very well indeed to match the canniness of wee Jackie.

What the drivers really need is someone with the shrewdness and strength of character of a Bernie Ecclestone, and so too do the motorcycle people.

The ill-fated motorcycle World Series which Kenny Roberts and journalist Barry Coleman tried to arrange in 1980 as a rival to the official FIM (Fédèration Internationale de Motocyclisme) 500cc Championship, foundered largely due to the absence of a sufficiently resourceful 'wheeler-dealer'. To run their races, Roberts and Co had to get the FIM at least partly on their side which they failed to do. In a head-on confrontation the FIM simply said, 'We refuse to sanction the series,' and the cause was lost. The fact that Barry Sheene, Virginio Ferrari and the majority of the top riders were in full favour of the new set-up (for there was theoretically far more money in it for them) made no difference. The FIM saw the series as a direct rival to their own Championship, which it was; they also looked upon the whole idea as an attempt by the riders to blackmail circuits into paying out more prize money, and they simply 'pulled the plug out'.

Had the matter been thought out differently, a mutually acceptable solution might have been found. The riders wanted a better financial arrangement, which was fair enough, and at the same time they wanted to cut out certain tracks on the grounds of safety. Unfortunately for them, the FIM controls all circuit licences and no organiser dared to 'go it alone' for fear of being refused permission to stage other events. It would have been a bit like a British circuit trying to run races without the agreement of the RAC.

I have enormous sympathy with the riders because I fear they will wait in vain for an Ecclestone-style 'FOCA' to emerge. The bike factories did not, in fact, support the World Series idea, which itself was a big blow. On top of that there are so many motorcyclists competing in so many categories – all of them with their own official 'World Championships', right down to

50cc – that proper control of all of them must be impossible to achieve.

For all these reasons, I can see that motorcycle racing is even more difficult to organise well than motor racing. Grand Prix drivers may still have their problems but, thanks to Ecclestone's astuteness, their sport is sufficiently rich to provide reasonable incomes even for the lesser lights. They are much better off financially than the vast majority of their two-wheeled fellows, although they race less often. The autocratic dictatorship of the French-based organising body of motorcycle racing indeed has a lot to answer for.

Not surprisingly, it can be said that top motorcyclists are rather more militant than top racing drivers. There has often been a lot of talk amongst drivers of boycotting an event due to a shortfall in safety precautions, but no F1 Grand Prix has so far been run without the participation of most of the top names. The nearest to a true walkout was the Spanish GP of 1975 (after I had retired from motor racing), the details of which Stirling recounts. Everyone started but Emerson Fittipaldi. However, at Spa, host to the Belgian motorcycle Grands Prix in 1979, the top 20 or so 500cc riders refused point blank to race over the revised circuit because the newly laid surface was 'sweating' and proving dangerously slippery. I wasn't there so I can't honestly say whether their complaints were justified or not, but at least the riders stuck to their guns and pulled out. They tried to compromise, too. Had the FIM agreed to 'demote' the 500cc Grand Prix, so that it did not count towards the World Championship, the top men would still have taken part. Predictably, the FIM would not agree to this and so Sheene, Roberts and the rest absented themselves. However, there was still a 'second division' of riders, men who normally would have had little hope of getting into the top places, who were only too eager to take part. With their much faster rivals spurning the contest, this was their chance for fame – if not fortune!

Aye, and there's the rub. Kenny Roberts, World 500cc Motorcycle Champion, may be able to get the top half of the grid on his side, but never the whole of it. There will always be plenty of new young hopefuls who will be prepared to ride no matter what.

Formula One fields, on the other hand, are only 24 strong and the same band of drivers take part in every race. Ecclestone has organised it that way, thus benefiting constructors and drivers while at the same time offering a virtual guarantee to the organisers that the cream of the world's drivers will take part every time.

And so far as representing the corporate view of the contestants is concerned, things are very much easier for Scheckter than for Roberts.

As an ex-rider and an ex-driver I naturally support both kinds of 'animal'. I know how easy it is for those in the firing line of both sports to be unwittingly manipulated by those controlling the purse-strings. I'm in favour of 'driver power', or 'rider power', because if the men whose very lives are at stake are not entitled to have a big say in the way things are run, then who is?

6 Going out and coming back

STIRLING MOSS

The circumstances of my Easter Monday crash at Goodwood in 1962 have been amply documented. The only thing missing is a definite, watertight reason for the accident. I've got my own theory, one I've not allowed to be published before, which I'll come on to in a moment. But whatever its true cause, the fact is that the shunt terminated my career as a Grand Prix driver and thus altered my whole life.

The real question mark in my mind is not so much why I crashed as whether, after my recovery, I made the decision to retire too soon. I was in hospital for months following the accident and I had some pretty bad injuries. Normally, however, racing drivers and racing motorcyclists recover incredibly swiftly from broken bones and so on, and I don't think I was an exception. When I crashed at Spa in 1960 I suffered crushed vertebrae, two broken legs and a broken nose. Yet I missed only three Grands Prix and was racing again inside two months.

The Goodwood business was different. I had smashed up my left side and was paralysed for six months. I was unconscious for one month and during my recovery – a slow, tedious business which went on right through 1962 and beyond – it was obvious that my co-ordination was not going to return in the same way that a bone re-fuses. It was not until just over a year after the shunt that I climbed back into a racing car, but even that period of time might not have been enough. I did about half an hour of running around the same Goodwood circuit driving a 2½-litre Lotus 19 sports car. The road was damp and I think I got to within a couple of seconds, maybe less, of what I considered to be a competitive time. But I knew almost immediately that things were not as they should have been; I was getting the car around reasonably quickly, but I was doing nothing instinctively. My concentration had gone. What had come automatically before now became a conscious effort. I would be going down the straight and suddenly find myself in the braking area without realising it. I would think, 'God, I should be braking by now,' and start to panic. Obviously, because I had raced so much I knew what to do when I thought about doing it. But because none of it came *without* thinking I decided it would be dangerous to myself and to others to make a return to racing. I was a man looking for a shunt.

After the test I sat down with my father and manager Ken Gregory and decided to make the announcement that I would retire from racing. There was a temptation, I suppose, to drop down a couple of leagues and keep racing in, say, touring cars. But the problem of concentration would still have been there and it was easy to see how one could kill oneself at a relatively slow speed as well as at a high speed. On top of that I did feel that by taking part in a less demanding form of motor racing I would only be half doing the job. I *have* now made a return to touring cars and historics but this I look upon completely differently. I have no ambition to make my name as a racing driver all over again and in particular I have no desire whatsoever to return to Formula One. Nineteen years must take their toll and clearly I could never be as good today as I was at the age of thirty-two.

Whether I should have persevered and made more of an effort to make a comeback in the sixties is another matter. I do, in fact, regret not delaying my test another six months or a year, perhaps even two years. By that time my concentration had largely returned and looking back I do believe that I could have made it. I would have been out of racing for perhaps a couple of seasons, but technology had not changed the cars unduly and I'm sure I could have adapted to the required technique without much difficulty. For instance, if I had made a comeback in 1965 the formula would have been the same and I would have been racing cars of similar power and handling characteristics to the one in which I crashed. Although rim widths had grown slightly by then, the wheels were still pretty narrow and slick tyres were unheard of. Later, when it dawned on me that perhaps I *had* made a mistake in abandoning the sport so soon, things were different. This would have been about five years after the shunt when the engine size had doubled and tyres were already adopting steamroller proportions. I would have jumped right in at the deep end without having learnt the new way to swim.

I think it's easy, as a racing driver, to cope with design changes as they happen. Wide wheels, slick tyres, wings, aerofoils, ground effect are all examples of major developments in racing car technology. If you are driving a car regularly it's no problem – or it shouldn't be if you are any good at all – to adapt to something new. In 1969 there was the business of wing breakages which caused the CSI suddenly to ban high-mounted aerofoils. The rules were actually changed half-way through practice for the Monaco Grand Prix and there was a lot of speculation that the cars would be undriveable, but in the event all that happened was that the drivers adapted their styles instinctively to cope with the problem. The fact that overnight they were denied the benefit of wings was of little concern to them once they took to the track. Similarly, I'm sure that none of today's top men had any difficulty at all in dealing with the huge extra downforce created by modern ground effect designs. If you are a new boy on the way up, driving a Formula One car for the first time is obviously going to be a daunting and difficult business but at least time is on your side. But for someone with his name already established, a return to top-level racing after a gap of five or seven years would, I'm sure, be sheer folly. To have gone back then as myself, with everybody expecting me to win, would have presented an impossible burden.

One thing I can say is that my decision to retire, and subsequently to remain retired, was in no way influenced by the mysterious circumstances of my accident. If my memory of the incident had returned to reveal it as being my fault, it would have made no difference. As it is I cannot remember the crash, or even the race (the last thing I can recall doing that day was to take a friend of mine round the paddock, before the racing started), and frankly I have no great desire to do so. What I have done is to piece together as much information as I can in an effort to deduce the most likely cause. It's not something I lie awake at nights worrying about, but naturally I am curious as to what really happened.

As is well known, I was driving a Lotus 'special' which was owned jointly by Rob Walker and the British Racing Partnership. The chassis, designed originally to take the standard Coventry-Climax 4-cylinder engine of the previous year, had been modified to accept the latest V8 Climax engine which gave a lot more power. (We already had a new Lotus on order, one purpose-built to take the V8, but it had yet to arrive.) As might have been expected, reliability with such a home-built machine was a problem; the thing was quite fast but in the two races prior to Goodwood we had suffered from broken valve gear and then broken throttle linkage. At Snetterton, one week before the Easter weekend, the throttle problem cost me the race; I was forced to make several pit-stops and had to settle for breaking the lap record. At Goodwood I had apparently found myself in a similar situation. This time the gearchange linkage was playing up and again I was forced into the pits. The mechanism was finally fixed and I returned to the race several laps adrift. I had no chance of winning but I imagine the lap record was what I was aiming for.

Trying to put all the known information together afterwards, it seems that what happened was this. I was behind the race leader, Graham Hill in a BRM, and catching up. Naturally I would have been keen to unlap myself if only to show that I could go as fast as him. We were negotiating the long right-hander at Fordwater, a corner which I could, and apparently did, take flat out. Graham may not have seen me, but I believe the flag marshal probably did and he would have shown Graham the blue flag to signal I was there. Graham in turn might have raised his hand in acknowledgement and I might have seen this and mistaken it for a sign for me to pass. Certainly I recall (from the previous day's practice) that Graham had taken a different line at this point, being further over to the right than I would be. If he had held that line, there would have been room for me to go through on the left, i.e. on the outside. If Graham had not intended me to go by, however, he would have moved over to the left-hand side of the road because this, under normal circumstances, would have been the usual thing to do; that would have been the regular racing line. I would thus have been faced with the BRM coming over and edging me towards the grass. This in itself might not have been disastrous, but there were a few ruts and hollows in the rough ground at the circuit edge and it would have been an easy thing to hit one of them and lose control.

All this is speculative, but based on the fact that immediately after the accident – or rather, immediately after Graham had won the race – he went up to my family and said, 'Look, I'm most awfully sorry, I had no idea that Stirling was going to pass me there'. It inferred that maybe he had pulled across on to me and I am bound to say that this does, to me, seem the most likely of all the theories.

Of course, there could have been a different reason. The car could have failed in some way, sending me off the track. If so, why has no evidence of any breakage prior to the crash ever been found? Alternatively, I could have made a mistake – and maybe I did. On the other hand, it is, I like to think, uncharacteristic of me to have made a mistake at such a high speed. It may sound strange, but whenever I did make mistakes I made sure they happened at a relatively slow speed like 70, 80 or perhaps 90. Then I could usually do something about it or, if not, the result would probably be nothing more serious than a spin. But to make a mistake at 140 is something else again – and, as I say, Fordwater was flat out as far as I was concerned, every lap the same. It was a fast part of the circuit, but it was not the most difficult or demanding part. St Mary's, the left-hander which followed, was very demanding and if I had gone off there I would most likely have blamed myself because at that time the corner was one of the trickiest around. As it was, we hadn't even reached the braking point for St Mary's.

I was left with several legacies from the accident, one or two of which remain even now. For example, I have to get up in the middle of the night to use the toilet. It may sound a small thing, but it's annoying to me because I'm the sort of person who can't get back to sleep very easily. The last thing of any importance which reminded me that I had taken quite a knock was the fact that for years I could not balance on my left foot. I was unable to do so for some twelve or thirteen years after the crash and I feel that my balance generally is still not as it should be - or was before Goodwood. When I waterski, for instance, my feeling of confidence is diminished when monoskiing on my left foot. None of this, however, affects my driving today.

Any consideration of an abbreviated career like mine begs the question, how long could he or she have gone on had the accident which put a stop to him or her not happened? I believe that so long as a driver moves along with the sport he can carry on at the top for very much longer than most currently do. What is lacking at the moment is incentive. There's bags of incentive to move up the ladder, but once the top couple of rungs are reached and the money starts roaring in, the pressure swiftly becomes so great as to put out the fire. I wanted to continue racing for as long as possible because I liked doing it; money was very much a secondary consideration, because, as I've explained, there wasn't so much of it about.

Physically and mentally, I don't see any reason why Formula One drivers shouldn't be able to go on to 50. Fangio retired at 47 and was over 40 when he won the first of his five world titles. By 1958 some of his best friends in racing had been killed and others had retired. I think he felt that perhaps he had had enough, that he had nothing left to prove - which in a way was right. Yet, I'm certain he could have gone on easily for another three or four seasons, just as I believe that Mario Andretti could go on for another 10 years. I think that perhaps Andretti, now already in his forties, *will* keep going until he's 50 - not in Grand Prix racing perhaps but in Indianapolis-style racing, which was his first love. He's the sort of driver for whom money is not everything (even though he's a multi-millionaire) and who keeps racing simply because he's in love with the sport. He's a driver who, were he to suffer a setback tomorrow, would bounce back the day after. He's not looking for new ways to enjoy life, motor racing still manages to give him what he needs. In that respect, he belongs to an older school of drivers, the one with which I am associated.

Vittorio Brambilla is another who you know will never pack it in while he can still run near the top. He was badly injured in the Ronnie Peterson accident at Monza in 1978 and at 40 years of age he might well have decided to quit while he was still alive. He had fractured his skull and for quite a while he was on the danger list. A year later what do we find? Vittorio Brambilla entered for the Italian Grand Prix in a blood-red Alfa Romeo, and going as well as ever!

Nor was I surprised when Niki Lauda came back after his fiery crash at the Nurburgring in 1976. At that time he felt he still had a lot to do – like win the Championship. He lost it that year to James Hunt, by a single point, but showed his mettle by coming back again in 1977 to beat everyone. Later, as further success eluded him, he seemed to lose interest, switching his allegiance to flying. His basic interest, it would seem, was not so much in motor racing as in twentieth century technology and how to master it. Once aircraft grabbed his attention, racing cars took a back seat.

Mike Hailwood, I'm sure, would have returned to F1 racing after his Nurburgring shunt had his injuries not forbidden it. It's entirely typical of him that, having realised he could still ride a racing motorcycle, he set his sights on the Isle of Man. I like to think I would have done the same.

David Purley is another who has made a comeback against all the odds (although predictably if you happen to know the man). Having been out of it for a couple of years, and with injuries that would make the average bloke scared of getting on to a bus, I'm not sure that David is being particularly clever in bidding to break back into Grand Prix racing, but you can't fault his style. Like Andretti, like Hailwood, he's a real racer who just can't stand being tied to the sidelines.

On the other hand, there are those drivers who are clearly not likely to bash on until they are even 40, let alone 50. For all his natural brilliance, I feel that Jody Scheckter's exit will coincide with his making his sixth million rather than winning his sixth Championship. His is the 'modern' approach, the super-professional approach, which carries with it a definite time limit. In fact it would not surprise me at all if he has retired from the game by the time this book is published.

Emerson Fittipaldi shows no sign of chucking in the towel, despite all his setbacks with the car, and that's immensely encouraging. Emerson could have driven for almost anybody, but decided instead to build his own car. There's real dedication involved there.

Coming back after a period away from racing, especially if you have been seriously injured, always involves a certain amount of nervousness. I don't believe that there has ever been a racing driver who knows no fear, and getting back into a sport which two or three months ago might nearly have killed you does take a degree of courage. When I raced for the first time after my Spa crash I found myself in Portugal, competing over a real road circuit with kerbs, pavements and trees. It was a super circuit, but I remember going through one section at about 120 mph or thereabouts and thinking, 'Boy, if that wheel comes off now I am in trouble'. There is no doubt that at moments like that you really begin to twitch. The only way from my point of view to cope with that was to get on with the job in hand, to concentrate on what I was doing and say to myself, 'OK, let's try and win this race'. I knew the feeling well, because I have probably had more mechanical failures - more wheels falling off (seven), more brake failures (eight), more steering columns sheared (two), more suspension failures (too many to remember) - than anyone else. Every time I sat in a racing car there was a good chance some part of it would break, but if I had started to ponder on these things while I was going through a difficult corner, whether it was at Silverstone or in the Mille Miglia, I simply could not have stood the strain. The only time I did not have to worry was while I was driving for Mercedes - they simply did not break, and nor generally did Ferraris, then as now.

Whatever the length of time away from the tracks, whatever personal problems one may have, there is one motive for returning to racing which must be resisted - money. How pleased I was when Jackie Stewart, having been offered an enormous sum of money by Bernie Ecclestone to make a comeback in 1979, turned it down! Like Hunt, Stewart's reason for retiring at the end of 1973 was that of survival. Under those circumstances, especially, it would be pointless, hypocritical even, to attempt a comeback. Money can't buy happiness. It's true that you can be comfortable and miserable when you've got money instead of being just miserable, but no amount of money would ever have lured me back into Formula One racing, not while I felt the task was beyond me. In Jackie's case, he actually gave up one race earlier than he intended when his team-mate, François Cevert, was killed in a shocking accident at Watkins Glen in 1973. Not surprisingly, that was all too much for Stewart then and, while time may have dulled the shock of Cevert's death, the fact remains that he retired because he had had enough of racing. I do not criticise the man for this, indeed I applaud his decision. He had the courage of his convictions and made the right choice. The circumstances were clearly exceptional and he could, after all, have given up two races earlier, after the Italian Grand Prix. Jackie clinched his third world title in that event and had he so chosen, he could have stopped there and then, as Niki Lauda did after winning the 1977 title. Stewart clearly recognised his obligation to the Tyrrell team and elected to do the final Grands Prix in Canada and the United States. Obviously, there were financial incentives as well, but then Jackie hardly needed the money. And money, as I say, is the last 'carrot' a top driver should ever consider.

I often wonder how long I would have continued in Grand Prix racing had I not shunted. It's a difficult question to answer. I had always said, and I meant it, that if ever I found other people quicker than myself in the corners, the places that mattered, then I would get out. All my career, practically without exception, I started every race in a car that was slower than the others down the straight. I always had to slipstream to keep up and I tried to regain lost time through braking later and cornering harder. It was the way I raced because it was the way I had to race if I wanted to win. I always felt I was taking more out of myself than out of the car and I'm sure that I would have been very quickly aware of any loss of ability. Quite simply, then, I would have carried on until other guys were faster or until I could see that I was physically not strong enough to carry the weight of the competition.

Whether I had reached my peak at the time of my accident is another tricky point, although I happen to believe that a driver should be capable of carrying his 'peak' along with him. Obviously there comes a time when a man has to admit he is past his best, but I don't see that a racing driver automatically gets slower just because he's reached 37, or even 47 years of age. I was only 32 when I was forced out and I like to think that my 'peak' hadn't yet been reached. Or if it had, that I could have taken it along consistently for many more years. Fangio was 47 when he retired and I firmly believe that he was just as good then as when he started. I don't think today's drivers give up because they are 'over the hill', but rather because they have had enough of a sport which no longer offers the fun and games it once did.

I don't believe there has ever been a case in motor racing of a competitor returning to the top echelon of the sport after having officially 'retired'. Some have come back successfully after injury, however, and clearly the shorter time you are away from the circuit the better. In cases like Lauda after his Nurburgring crash, or Fangio after his big shunt at Monza, or myself after Spa, the idea of 'retirement' never occurred to us. As far as we were concerned we were simply taking a spot of sick leave. I imagine that Mike thought the same way after he shunted at the Ring in 1974. He did appear to abandon all hopes of racing again once he realised the severity of his injuries and I'm surprised it didn't occur to him earlier that, if he was physically unable to race a car, then what was wrong with his first love - motorcycles? I presume that he felt too much water had gone under the bridge since he last raced a bike and that the machinery and the mode of riding had changed too much. I'm sure I would have felt this, but Mike was fortunate in that technology in the world of motorcycle racing advances at a much slower rate than it does in the world of cars. Bikes really have developed at snail's pace over the years with the result that Mike probably found even the 500cc full-race Suzuki much closer to the sort of thing he used to ride in the sixties than he had anticipated. Today's F1 cars, on the other hand, are pulling a lateral g-factor of 2.9 whereas at the end of my career the cornering force probably wasn't above 0.9 g, and this alone makes a tremendous difference to the feel of the car. Mike, in returning to bikes, did not have this barrier to step over and despite the timelag of eleven years, he was good enough to bridge the gap and learn all over again.

There's one final thing that particularly upsets me about being out of racing during the sixties and seventies. It is that I could no longer bring my experience to bear in the way the sport has evolved, both technically and politically. Had I continued, I'm sure that I would have been able to find a nucleus of guys – Andretti, Brambilla, drivers of that sort – strong, good and fast, who could have been swayed to my way of thinking in terms of development.

Motor racing has been forced to take certain routes, not all of them desirable in my opinion. The colour is still there. The excitement is still there. The urgency is still there and so is the sense of occasion. But the freedom of enjoyment has been undermined. And the danger zones are deeper and wider. I do like to believe that had I been able to make an immediate comeback in 1962 and 1963, I might also have been able to act as a moderating influence – to have helped prevent some of the changes in the sport from being so dramatic.

MIKE HAILWOOD

A lot of folk imagine that it's a natural progression for a motorcycle racer eventually to turn to cars, so let me tell them, it's a lot harder than it looks! I made the mistake in the sixties of trying to combine the two – by 1963 I had won a couple of World Championships on bikes and I was ready for something new. On the other hand, I had no intention of abandoning bike racing – it was what I did best and it was essential, financially, to continue.

Breaking into car racing seemed like a good idea at the time. I suppose I imagined that I had proved myself on bikes so I had to show off in another area! I was king of the kids and ready to demonstrate to the world how to drive a racing car. Unfortunately, it was all a bit of a 'floperoo'.

Not that I immediately jumped in at the deep end. Before I could attack the Grand Prix scene I had to qualify for an international licence which meant doing a few smaller-scale races. I decided to order a Formula Junior Brabham. Formula

Junior was the forerunner of modern-day Formula Three and the Brabham seemed the best car around at the time. I went down to the works the night before my first race at Brands Hatch and of course the thing wasn't ready. I hung around until all hours, eventually transporting the car down to Brands early on race-day morning and grabbing a couple of hours sleep in the wagon. I remember while I was waiting for the car to be finished having to listen to a very severe lecture from Ron Tauranac, Jack Brabham's partner. He seemed quite annoyed that I should have gone to them in the first place. 'We sell these things to all you young so-and-so's just so that you can write them off and give us a bad name!' he moaned.

I thought, 'Here am I spending two or three thousand pounds on one of your cars and here are you telling me how I should drive it and what I should do.' But I think Ron gave every one of his customers the same treatment; he obviously didn't have much faith in us young bloods!

I didn't do all that badly in the Brabham, which was bright yellow as I recall. I had a fifth, a fourth, a couple of seconds and a couple of wins and I thought, 'Phew, you're ready for the big time, baby!' As I've already mentioned, I then sort of bought my way into Reg Parnell's Formula One team, quickly to discover I wasn't another Fangio after all. To be fair on myself, it wasn't all my fault that success was not forthcoming. The Parnell cars had BRM engines which were never much good (BRM themselves never found time to service the things) and we also suffered terribly from gearbox problems which were never solved. After a couple of years I got fed up with it and went back to bikes. I had already found that the car racing was getting in the way of the bike racing, and through constantly running into trouble on four wheels my morale was suffering even when I went back to two.

I was also put off cars somewhat by the social attitude which prevailed generally. Although I joined in and thoroughly enjoyed a lot of the revelry that went on, I was conscious of a certain antagonism from the car racing set. Bike racers just weren't accepted in those days. The car scene was a very closed shop and motorcyclists were looked down upon as complete interlopers. The class distinction was very much greater then than it is today and it was difficult to get people to take you seriously. Ask John Surtees. He had a really hard time breaking into the car world, despite all his brilliance. In his case, particularly, I think many of the established stars of Formula One resented someone coming in from what they felt was an inferior sport and showing them the way.

For three years or so I went back to bikes full-time. Then in 1968 Honda, for whom I had been riding, pulled out of bike racing which left me with not a lot to do. Soon, I again found myself mixed in with people from car racing – Paul Hawkins, Malcolm Guthrie and various others who were quite heavily into sports car events. It wasn't long before I was sucked back into motor racing, only this time I wasn't really aiming to beat the world, just to do as well as I could. I was virtually starting again from scratch, but without the complication of racing bikes full-time as well. I did ride in a few bike races in '68, but once Formula 5000 started in 1969, I concentrated solely on cars.

When I found myself back in Formula One in 1971 I think I was a bit surprised, but pleased nevertheless. Not too many people get a second bite of the cherry! And oddly enough my car racing career seemed to have much in common with that of another 'Ditton Road Flyer', Peter Revson. Revvie had raced a bit in the States before coming over to Europe in the early sixties and joining Chris Amon and myself at Parnell's. While Chris moved on to greater things with Ferrari, Peter and I disappeared from the Grand Prix circuits at about the same time. I always figured I was faster than Revvie in those early days but when he returned to Formula One in the seventies *he* was the guy who started winning races, not me! In the end, of course, I proved luckier. Sadly, Peter was killed early in 1974 while testing a Shadow at Kyalami, South Africa.

Having re-established myself in Formula One, I was determined to make the best of the opportunity. Contrary to popular opinion, I took it as seriously as I was able of taking anything seriously, and certainly I was anxious to make as big a success of it as I could. My greatest difficulty was coping with the technical side. In this area, bike racing was always far more straightforward than car racing. Basically, you didn't need to know very much about the design of a bike to make it go fast.

Cars, on the other hand, have always been much more sophisticated and I'm ashamed to say that I really didn't go out of my way to learn. I wasn't very attentive or retentive as far as the art of chassis tuning was concerned!

Still, we had flashes of brilliance here and there in 1972 when I was driving what was arguably the best-ever Formula One Surtees, the TS9B. But the following year proved a total disaster. The cars were never any good, and three of them - the complete team - were written off in one enormous accident at Silverstone. That was the occasion when a very green Jody Scheckter spun his McLaren at Woodcote on the opening lap right in front of everybody. My Surtees, plus those of Carlos Pace and Jochen Mass, were among eight or nine cars which were badly damaged.

But in any case the car rarely held together for more than about five minutes at a time and I realised that for the following season I had to make the break from John's team. He had served me well and I like to think I had done the best job I could, but I saw that if I was to find real success in Grand Prix racing I had to load the odds in my favour - and that meant driving the best available car.

To start with, the 1974 season went well. Driving the Yardley-sponsored but factory-prepared McLaren M23, I chalked up quite a few points over the early races. In Argentina, I was a little fortunate to finish fourth after a stone had punctured the water radiator, and in Brazil I arrived home fifth with my arms falling off (the front tyres had developed a shocking vibration which made it murder to steer). In South Africa I suffered more vibration problems but managed to finish third and suddenly I was lying equal second in the World Championship, one point behind Regazzoni and level with Hulme, Fittipaldi and Reutemann. Unfortunately, at this point my luck started to run out. I finished out of the points in Spain and in Belgium a fuel pick-up problem robbed me of fifth place, although I must admit I had spun earlier. At Monaco, I managed to dodge all the first lap chaos - seven cars were eliminated after a multiple shunt going up the hill towards the Casino - only to slide off into the Armco eleven laps later while lying fifth. In Sweden I went out even earlier with fuel starvation and my standing in the points table was now a lowly ninth!

In Holland I recouped a bit of lost ground by finishing fourth, right on Fittipaldi's tail but well adrift of the two Ferraris of Lauda and Regazzoni. The French Grand Prix at Dijon brought me no further reward – I ended up seventh – while at Brands Hatch I lost another fifth place when I spun; the engine was already overheating and it refused to fire up, so I was out.

The next race, little did I know it, was to be my last. Ironically, it was one I looked forward to most: the German Grand Prix over the Nurburgring. Practice at the Ring is always a difficult business. There is never enough time to learn the circuit properly and yet at the same time one is hesitant about embarking on a lap of the 14-mile plus course until the car is set up properly. The result is that a lot of people spend much of their time going round and round the short pits loop. On the other hand, it is vital to set a decent time during the first day's practice since you can never be sure it isn't going to rain the following day.

As usual I had the choice of two chassis, and I was pressing on in the one I preferred when, entering the chicane at the end of the Ring's one and only straight, a front wishbone broke and pitched me into the guardrail. I was OK – this time – but the car was a goner, at least for this race. The next day I was forced to switch to the spare car but before I could get down to a really good time the sky darkened and the rain began to spit down, swiftly turning into a steady downpour. All this meant that my grid position had to come from the previous day, the time established before the shunt. I found myself back on the sixth row, alongside Tom Pryce in his Shadow. At the front were the two Ferraris, then Fittipaldi in the number one McLaren and Scheckter in the Tyrrell. Immediately ahead of me was my team-mate from the previous year, Jochen Mass, still with Surtees, and Jacky Ickx driving a Lotus. Also ahead of me were Depailler, Reutemann, Hulme and Peterson, so I knew I had a lot to do if I was to get into the points.

The start was a complete shambles. The two works McLarens hit each other causing Hulme's immediate retirement, while at the left-hander behind the pits Lauda collided with Scheckter, leaving the Ferrari stranded amid the catch fencing. Denny tried to restart using his spare car, but was immediately disqualified, and when Emerson also packed it in, his car too damaged to continue, mine was the only McLaren left in the race. From twelfth place on the grid I quickly found myself eighth behind Ickx (Lotus), Depailler (Tyrrell) and Peterson (Lotus). Patrick and Ronnie were having an incredible battle, which ended when the Frenchman locked a wheel and crashed. This left me in seventh place, trying to catch the two Lotuses and also Jochen Mass, who was driving superbly on his home circuit.

After ten of the fourteen laps poor Jochen disappeared with engine failure. This left me scrapping with the two John Player Lotuses and I remember feeling pretty pleased with myself when I passed Ronnie. He had also crashed in practice and was driving the newer-model Lotus which was never a success. Even so, he was regarded as the quickest driver around in those days and at the Nurburgring the car was not (at that time) as important as the driver. I was also catching Ickx for fourth place, which I felt chuffed about because Jacky was the acknowledged 'Ringmaster', having won the Grand Prix for both Brabham and Ferrari. So there we were, locked together in this great old dice, when I suddenly found myself heading straight for the barrier at the Pflanzgarten. This is where all the cars become airborne as the road drops sharply away and it's important to land straight; the road isn't straight, but *you* have to be. As it was, I landed cockeyed. I might have been a bit tired, but if I'm completely honest the reason I got myself in such a predicament was due purely and simply to brain fade! There was the inevitable theory that something had broken, but afterwards the car was so smashed that it was impossible to see what might have failed - there really wasn't much of it left. For my money, though, it was all down to me.

Feeling it was my fault hardly helped at the time, of course. Once the car had landed sideways, it shot straight for the Armco and, although I managed to sit hard on the brakes, we were still doing about 110 mph by the time I clobbered the rail. The car hit forwards at an acute angle, then slammed its way down the road with bits flying off everywhere. I don't think Ronnie missed me by much and it must have been a very dodgy moment for him. The impact into the Armco did my right leg and foot no good at all. The leg was broken just below the knee joint and the suspension came back into the cockpit and squashed the foot. On top of that the sheer force of the collision flattened the heel and pushed the heel bone up into the ankle bone. I remained conscious throughout the rescue operation, which again was no help because it hurt like mad! I was taken to Adenau Hospital where I spent an anxious couple of days before being flown back to London and installed in St Thomas's. I was in hospital only a relatively short time – a couple of weeks or so – but I subsequently had two operations on the foot and although the plan was to get fit enough to race in the last couple of events in North America, there simply was no way. My foot was too mangled to operate the pedals. All I could be thankful for was that I was still alive. Had I been driving anything but the McLaren, which was a particularly strong car, I'm positive it would have been curtains. As for the safety precautions at the Ring, all I can say is that had there been more of a run-off area, or perhaps some catch fencing, the impact obviously would not have been so severe. But if the Armco had not been there at all I would have gone down among the trees, which could have been very nasty indeed.

After the accident I soon realised that there was no way I could ever again race a car. Even driving an ordinary car was difficult, and still is up to a point, because I had no up and down movement at the ankle. To use the accelerator I have to push with my whole leg. To be honest, I don't think I was terribly disappointed. I was very fed up about the injury, naturally, but knowing I could not continue racing in a way came as something of a relief. I wasn't really enjoying it and now I had a cast-iron excuse to stop. It seems a pity to look upon it in that way but it happens to be the truth. Mark you, had the accident not occurred I suppose I might still have been going now. I don't think I would have become any faster, but since racing was what I was best at I doubt if I would have given up voluntarily. At the time, I couldn't imagine doing anything else. After 16 years or so, the bug of racing had bitten so deep that it was becoming harder, not easier, to think of quitting.

In the end, therefore, the Nurburgring shunt perhaps did me a favour. Had it not happened, I would have gone on and on and might have been dead by now. One has to look on the bright side!

Of course, I had much to regret. It was the end of an era, if one can put it that way, and I had failed to win a single Formula One race. I was 34 and cut off, as it were, in my prime. Nor had I made a fortune. One compelling reason to continue racing was that of money and at that stage I hadn't earned nearly enough. Today, whereas many drivers *could* continue until they're grey-haired, most tend to start younger and give up younger. As in any sport, the trend is to reach the top earlier. And if you find yourself a rich man by the age of 25 why not say, 'OK, I've had enough'?

For myself, a change of scene was called for and I disappeared from the circuits for a few years to set up home in New Zealand. Gradually, however, the old bug began to re-emerge. Having one more big go entered my mind more and more often. Twit that I am, I must insist that the initial idea of returning to the Isle of Man was mine. Having abandoned any idea of car racing, I reverted to the bike world. In 1977 the ACU invited me over to Silverstone for the motorcycle British Grand Prix - just to be driven around the track. Not to put too fine a point on it, the fans went bananas just at the sight of me in the back of a car and I thought, 'Well, if they're still that keen I'll have to see what I can do about having another go.' I had a chat with the ACU and they thought it was a good idea. We actually agreed then and there that I should race on the Isle of Man, assuming I could find suitable machinery and assuming too that I still felt the same way about it when the time came. I settled for the Island because I figured that, since no-one really tries that hard round the course - or shouldn't if they want to stay aboard - I stood a good chance of doing reasonably well despite the long lay-off. I realised that I would be quickly down the tubes if I tried to go Grand Prix racing, but I felt the Island would continue to be kind to me and that I could have a wobble round without disgracing myself. What I didn't realise was that the standard of riding on the Island had gone down in the intervening period. The TT no longer counted towards the Championship and many of the top riders – Barry Sheene, Kenny Roberts and so on – didn't bother with it, either because they didn't have to or because they didn't want to. Others found it too expensive an exercise and still more, while turning up to race, avoided spending enough time and money to practise properly. The result was that when I arrived I found that very few of the competitors knew the circuit in the way they should have done. And, again because of the fear of blowing up their bikes and incurring still more expense, they were trying less hard than I had expected. Consequently, there were very few who, firstly, really knew their way around and, secondly, were prepared to race hard.

I went over there with the intention of finishing in the top six, if I could. As things turned out I won the Production TT riding the Ducati and then failed abysmally in the remainder of the races. In the 500 and the Classic TTs my Martini-sponsored Yamahas let me down. In the 250 race, with conditions alternating between wet and dry, I'm afraid that I let the bike down because I just wasn't used to riding in the wet. So, although the opening race proved an unexpected triumph, the remainder of the week was a disaster. Over the months that followed, I felt in the back of my mind that I had disappointed a lot of people. Not through any fault of my own, maybe, but a fact nevertheless. An awful lot of folk had clearly gone across to see me ride and hadn't – not unless they had caught a glimpse of the Production race. So I thought, 'All right, for 1979 we'd better give it one more try.'

We went through the same routine as before, speaking to the ACU and chasing sponsors. Perhaps because this time I was less of a novelty, commercial backing was not so readily forthcoming. But Suzuki were kind enough to lend me a 500cc racer and in the end things worked out quite well. It was funny really, because when I went to Donington to test the bike I had been hearing such horrendous tales from Barry Sheene and Steve Parrish about how bad the Suzukis were that I was quite worried. I did a day's testing and the Suzuki people said, 'What do you want to have done with it?', perhaps thinking that I was going to tell them to throw it in the lake!

I said, 'Just take it away and spray it.' They were amazed, but in truth I found it better than the Yamahas the year before. Of course, I wasn't riding to the limits as were the likes of Sheene and Parrish, but it is true in racing that one man's poison is another's beef. All I knew was that the bike felt all right to me.

In addition to the Suzuki I had another Ducati for the Production TT which managed to lose about 10 horsepower somewhere along the way. It had also lost all its good handling from the year before and so we were in trouble with that right from the start. In the Senior TT, though, once a lot of people had fallen out, I managed to win fairly easily, finishing ahead of Scotsman Alex George. Oddly enough, in the other race, the Classic, although I tried very much harder, I was only tenths of a second quicker on the Suzuki. I missed winning it by three and a half seconds, which was a bit frustrating. But at least I'd achieved what I'd set out to do which was have another good go and win another TT. I did feel that I had no need to go back again.

Nevertheless, perhaps foolishly, I did agree to do a couple more smaller races in Britain. The first was at Mallory Park on a TT Formula One production machine which I had never ridden before - indeed it had never turned a wheel until that event - and which really wasn't up to much. In the race I started having trouble with the brakes and was happy to pack it in.

Really, that should have been my last effort. Since racing on the Island I had lost all interest. Before Mallory - indeed just before the TT itself - I had gone to Northern Ireland to watch the Northwest 200 in which Tommy Herron, team-mate to Sheene and Parrish in the Suzuki lineup, was killed. There were a whole load of other nasty accidents that day and then during practice at Mallory I saw a couple of guys fall off. In the old days I was more or less unaffected by other people's accidents, but now I found they were putting me right off.

I had, however, promised Tom Wheatcroft that I would do a 'farewell' race at his circuit, Donington. Frankly I hated the idea, but Tom had always been very good to me and I felt I owed him a favour. Even so, my heart wasn't in it and in practice I fell off at the fast left-hander going down the hill. It was silly because I wasn't trying for a quick lap or anything. In fact, I had no intention of riding flat out at any time and I don't think people expected me to race hard. I was merely set for a 'goodbye' appearance. Perhaps it was *because* I wasn't taking the business particularly seriously that I crashed. I wasn't interested and so I lost concentration, that's all I can think. I do know for sure that the sudden, hard contact between me and the road was as painful as anything I could remember. I had broken my collarbone and although I had it pinned up I was in no shape to race. So my great farewell ride eventually took place in the back of Tom's course car!

On reflection, I was pretty lucky to get away with it. Not just the Donington accident, but my comeback as a whole. I think I must have been crazy! I had really given up bikes when I started seriously in cars, and yet here I was trying to turn the clock back ten years. Up until the point when I competed in the 1977 TT, I knew I had it inside me that I wanted to do something more. I'm glad now that I did it, that I got it *completely* out of my system, but I can see all too clearly that it could have been a total disaster. There must be nothing worse than going through life feeling somehow that you haven't done everything you should, but in my case it can easily be argued that the risks were greater than the fulfilment.

Fortunately, it all turned out well. But I could so easily have been killed or seriously injured, neither of which would have done anyone any good, least of all me! I had perhaps expected to take a tumble somewhere along the line, but when I did it was somehow different to the way I remembered. Not only did it hurt more, but I felt completely helpless. This was brought home to me not just with the Donington crash, but also by an earlier one at Misano in Italy. We were testing the Ducati and for some reason known only to the Italians they had fitted the gearchange lever so that when you stepped on it it changed to a lower gear instead of a higher one – completely the reverse of the normal arrangement. For a couple of days I coped quite happily, but then got into a bit of a panic at one corner, found myself in neutral and stamped on the wretched lever to get a gear. On any other bike this would, as I say, have selected a higher gear; as it was I realised too late that I had changed down with the result that when I dropped the clutch the rear wheel locked and I was sent flying down the road.

I felt very second-hand indeed afterwards but what worried me most was that, despite having got myself really fit once again, feeling properly sharp, I seemed to have no control over events once I had 'lost it'. In the old days you would fall off, slide along and to a certain extent remain master of your destiny. But at Misano and also at Donington I retained no control of myself whatsoever, which was incredibly frightening. I just went tumbling down the road like a rag doll, arms and legs everywhere. Why, I'm not sure. Getting older, maybe, lacking some earlier instinct for survival, I just don't know. But the shunt in Italy certainly made me think and when I did it again, well, that was it!

I made the final decision as I was sailing through the air at Donington - just before I landed on my head! 'What the ------ am I doing here,' I thought. 'This is silly.' And after three hours on the operating table, my mind was made up. I just didn't care if I never so much as sat on a racing motorcycle again. Which is perhaps the way it should be when you retire from something as compelling as motorsport.

Let me clarify one point, however. While I would not recommend that anyone tries to do what I did, i.e. go back to 'serious' racing years after they have given up, I applaud Stirling in his return to saloon car racing. I fully understand that he, like me, has something to work out of his system. But while I know he will be trying as hard as he dares, saloon cars will not present the same dangers, or make the same demands, as single seaters - or indeed motorbikes. I hope that, by the time you read this, he will have burned the rest of them off the tracks; but even if he doesn't I'm sure he won't regret his decision to have one more go, just as I, despite all my misgivings, do not regret mine.

Finally, a word about Barry Sheene whose breakthrough into

the car world has often been rumoured. Barry is far and away the best racing motorcyclist Britain has had for years. He compares with any who have gone before him and I know that I am grateful that he wasn't riding when I was – I had enough trouble with Agostini! Because of his greatness, I sincerely believe he would be foolish to turn to four wheels. He's won two 500cc World Championships, which is good going, but I'm sure he can win some more. Before he abandons bikes in favour of cars I would like to see him recapture his Championship, lost to Kenny Roberts in '78 and '79, and do his best to dominate the two-wheeled scene.

Turning to cars is not necessarily the natural step for a motorcyclist to take. The technique is vastly different and there's much, much more to learn technically. John Surtees was able to make it and to a degree so was I. Others, like Agostini, have found it rather harder than maybe they anticipated and several, like Geoff Duke and John Hartle, didn't give themselves sufficient chance. It's a bit of a lottery.

From where I sit I can see that Sheene still has a lot to gain riding bikes; in cars perhaps he has rather more to lose.

7 My greatest races

STIRLING MOSS

In earlier books, notably *A Turn at the Wheel,* I have told the story of my most successful years in Grand Prix racing - 1957-60. Those years saw the rise of British Formula One teams from a position of near-obscurity to one of world domination. I was pleased and proud to have been associated with British cars during that period in which, driving either Vanwall, Cooper or Lotus, I won 11 Grandes Epreuves*. But successful as those seasons were (even if the World Championship continued to elude me) they did not include what I have always regarded as my two most satisfying victories. These occurred in 1961, my last full season in F1 racing and one in which British cars again had to play second fiddle to Ferrari.

The red cars were, on paper at least, unbeatable that year, with far greater horsepower than any other manufacturer could muster. But in two Grands Prix, in Monaco and Germany, I did manage to beat them and even now I often permit myself the

*The term 'Grande Epreuve', literally meaning 'Grand Test', was used during the fifties and sixties to describe rounds of the World Championship. In those days there were very many more Formula One races than are staged today, the majority of them non-Championship events. Many of those races took the title 'Grand Prix', being serious, full-blooded motor races without actually counting towards the title chase. Among the best known were the Syracuse Grand Prix, the Caen Grand Prix, the Reims Grand Prix and the Bordeaux Grand Prix. The term Grande Epreuve was introduced to distinguish between these events and the genuine World Championship Grands Prix. I won many 'Grands Prix' but only 16 'Grandes Epreuves'. Nowadays, with non-Championship F1 races having all but disappeared, the term has fallen into disuse and a Grand Prix is automatically assumed to be a Championship event.

luxury of savouring the memory. I enjoy recalling those races not just because I won (although obviously that's a very gratifying aspect!) but also because they prove a point, namely that in those days a performance advantage in another car could be overcome if the driver of an intrisically slower vehicle was prepared to have a go.

Throughout the '61 season I drove for Rob Walker, as I had the year before. The big difference was that the rules of Formula One had changed to allow engines of only 1½ litres capacity instead of the previous 2½ litres. This somewhat radical, and in my view retrograde, step had been signalled by the FIA as early as 1958 so all the teams had been given plenty of time to prepare themselves. The problem was that the British constructors had tended to disbelieve that such a sweeping change would indeed take place. They had also become side-tracked into supporting a rival series to F1, entitled the Intercontinental Formula, which allowed engines up to three litres. This obviously gave a new lease of life to the existing 2½-litre single-seaters and a few races for such cars *were* run during 1961. However, the anticipated support from Enzo Ferrari for the Intercontinental category proved over-optimistic and it soon became clear that the great man was, as ever, setting his sights firmly on winning the World Championship. His V6, mid-engined Dino 156 car was a development from the 1960 Formula Two car which was already known to be very fast. With the German Porsche firm also said to have a multi-cylindered car ready to go in F1, the British looked forward to the season with some dismay.

There was no great shortage of cars, because the previous year's 1½-litre F2 vehicles could be used in the new F1 with only minor changes. But the existing Coventry-Climax 4-cylinder engines on which, to start with, all the UK outfits depended (even BRM), produced only 140 bhp compared to the 190 bhp or so of the V6 Ferrari. Porsche proved slow in producing their 8-cylinder engine, but even so the proven flat-4 motor certainly gave more power than the Climax unit. Of course, both Climax and BRM had new designs on the drawing board, but for the majority of the year we were all stuck with the outmoded F2 engines and it was a question of like it or lump it.

A warning of what was to come was given in April at the non-Championship Syracuse Grand Prix in Sicily. All the major works teams were entered and I was there in Rob's Lotus 18. The incredible thing was that Ferrari chose Syracuse to make their '61 debut not only with the brand new car - which was a logical decision - but with a brand new driver - which was a bit of a surprise.

We were even more surprised when we saw how Ferrari's new man could go. The driver chosen, Formula Junior graduate Giancarlo Baghetti, qualified second fastest in practice, ahead of John Surtees in his Cooper and Graham Hill in his BRM. Only Dan Gurney's Porsche was faster, by a fifth of a second. My car did not run well all weekend - the engine had some kind of misfire as I remember - and I was never in contention. In the race, Baghetti drove like a hero and, after a wheel-to-wheel battle with Dan Gurney, won by five seconds. His victory was as astounding and unexpected as that achieved by my former team-mate Tony Brooks, who in 1955 had triumphed in the same race driving a British Connaught, thus recording the first GP win for a British car since Henry Segrave won the 1923 French Grand Prix in a Sunbeam.

The point about Baghetti's win was that if an unknown could beat the rest of us, what on earth would the proper works team of Phil Hill, Wolfgang von Trips and Richie Ginther do at Monte Carlo, scene of the opening round of the Championship? Certainly no-one expected Ferrari to be beaten at Monaco. They had finally been won over to the superior rear-engined concept and if the Dino chassis was not quite as good as my Lotus, it was clearly pretty capable and there was still that frightening power advantage about which we could do nothing.

There was another shock awaiting us when we arrived in Monte. Colin Chapman, the Lotus boss and the man who has time and again re-written the design engineer's handbook as far as Grand Prix cars are concerned, had set to over the winter building the successor to the Type 18 and at Monaco he wheeled out a pair of brand new Lotus 21 models for Jimmy Clark and Innes Ireland. As a customer, Rob naturally had to make do with his older, regular model. But almost as soon as practice started it was apparent that the new 'pencil line' factory cars with their lower, slimmer bodywork and revised suspension were potentially quicker than mine.

However, Innes crashed heavily during practice when he selected the wrong gear going through the tunnel and put himself in hospital with a broken leg. This reduced the opposition slightly, but it was obvious from practice that Monaco was going to be a very close, very hard motor race. I managed to qualify on pole with a time of 1 minute 39.1 seconds. Ginther, driving the only Ferrari fitted with the latest 120° V6 engine (as opposed to the Syracuse 65° units given to Phil Hill and von Trips), was a fifth of a second slower, with Clark's Lotus completing the front row. Graham Hill did well to equal Clark's time to claim a place on the second row in the BRM-Climax, just ahead of the other two Ferraris. A mere two seconds covered the first twelve drivers, but one had the feeling that Ferrari were playing a canny game: I certainly expected them to go faster in the race.

Because of the heat I had the side panels removed from my car, which at least gave the spectators a good view of what I was doing in the cockpit! The race was 100 laps in those days and was due to last two and three-quarter hours, so it was important to keep as cool as possible. (Today's Monaco Grand Prix, admittedly run over a slightly longer circuit, is just 76 laps long and is over inside two hours.) I was to congratulate myself on that decision by the end of the race.

I didn't make that good a start and both Ginther and Clark beat me to the Gasometer hairpin. Jo Bonnier in a Porsche also got going very quickly and for a while we had quite a dice. Clark soon dropped back with fuel pump trouble but as I watched the red tail of Ginther's car gradually getting further and further away I remember thinking, 'Boy, if I don't get away from Bonnier soon, Richie will have disappeared.'

We were racing as hard as we could even at this early stage, but I did manage to get rid of the Porsche to start reeling in Ginther's Ferrari. By lap twelve I had caught him and I suppose I could have stayed on his tail for quite some time. But I was mindful of the other Ferraris coming up behind and it seemed to me that the sooner I took the lead, the better. I slipped by on lap fifteen and managed to hold on thereafter – but what a struggle it was! Bonnier also slipped past Ginther, but for lap after lap it was a devil of a job to shake them off. Meanwhile Phil Hill had come through the field in his Ferrari and I knew that once either Richie or Phil got in front of the Porsche that I would be in real trouble again. I would look across at each hairpin and there the three of them would be, only yards behind. I was under greater mental pressure than in any race I can remember.

Once we got to lapping the back markers I was able to get away a tiny bit and when the Ferraris started fighting among themselves I managed, by half distance, to extend my advantage to nearly eight seconds. By this time Phil Hill had taken up the cudgels to lead the pursuit and there was never a moment when I could ease up even a fraction. I was convinced that sooner or later the Ferraris would again catch me, but all I could do was to press on as fast as possible. The Lotus was going like a train, never missing a beat, despite the pasting I was giving it. Alf Francis, my mechanic, had certainly screwed the thing together well that day.

As the race entered its last quarter, I was aware that Ginther had re-taken Hill and was closing. The Californian had obviously got his 'second wind' and on lap 84 he slashed three seconds from his best practice lap to put me firmly in his sights. There was no question of my allowing him to close up: I was already driving flat out, just as I had been from the start. At the line I was just 3.7 seconds in front with the two of us sharing fastest lap at 1 minute 36.3 seconds. Phil Hill finished third, 38 seconds further back, with von Trips trailing home fourth, two laps down. Bonnier had retired with fuel-injection problems after 59 laps.

I don't believe, in a race of that length, that I had ever before driven totally 'flat' from start to finish. But I did at Monaco in 1961, and I do look upon it as my most satisfying win of all. The only disappointment was that the organisers refused to hand out their customary prize for fastest lap. The lap record, which stood at 1 minute 36.2 seconds, had been set the year before by Bruce McLaren in a 2½-litre Cooper. Richie and I had lapped to within one-tenth of this time, despite our 1,000cc disadvantage. But because we hadn't actually broken the record, the organisers decided we weren't worthy of their award!

The other race that really pleased me that year was the German Grand Prix at the Nurburgring. Again, I was driving the Walker Lotus 18, now fitted with smoother bodywork and revised suspension. But in many ways the opposition was even tougher than it had been at Monaco. The Ferraris had got properly into their stride and had won the Dutch, Belgian, French and British Grands Prix. For the Ring they entered four cars: the regular trio of Hill, von Trips and Ginther plus Belgian Willy Mairesse. Willy was better known as a sports car driver but he was mightily quick, if totally unpredictable, in any sort of car. Porsche, Lotus and BRM were all there in strength but the big news from Cooper was that they had taken delivery of the first V8 Climax engine, one which gave as much power as the Ferraris. Jack Brabham was to drive this and in practice his time of 9 minutes 1.4 seconds was beaten only by Phil Hill, who had put in a phenomenal 'once in a lifetime' lap of 8 minutes 55.2 seconds. I was third quickest, three-tenths slower than Jack. Bonnier's Porsche was next, followed by the Ferrari of 'local hero' von Trips. Clark had written off one of the works Lotuses in practice and a lot of people had lurid moments on a track which was often wet in places.

This season Dunlop had introduced a new tyre intended for wet-track racing, the 'high hysteresis' D12. This was made of a softer compound than the regular dry-weather tyre and ran much 'hotter'. In the wet this was ideal, but once the track dried the rate of wear went up quite a lot. The D12s did, however, offer better adhesion in the dry. Race day dawned grey and unsettled and before the start there was a heavy downpour. The GT race which preceded the Grand Prix was run in the wet but by the time the F1 cars were wheeled out the track had virtually dried. Most of the teams, including Ferrari, opted to use the normal Dunlop D9 tyre. This was encouraging, because in my view the D12s could last the race even on a dry road and in any case there was every likelihood that some parts of the track would remain damp, or that it would rain again during the event. I don't think Dunlop was too happy about my choice, but I remained convinced that the gamble was worth taking; I was determined to take every opportunity I could of cancelling out the Ferrari power advantage and frankly on the D9s I couldn't see myself beating them.

In the panic before the start Brabham too decided on D12s only to find there was a set available only for his front wheels but not his rears. Thus he started with 'wets' on the front and 'dries' on the back. I led off the line and out into the forest, but we hadn't gone a mile before Jack came roaring past, the V8 Climax screaming merrily. He chopped in front of me in rather an ungentlemanly fashion, then spun straight off the road! He had found a damp patch under the trees, the D12s had gripped at the front but the rear end had lost adhesion immediately and his car rocketed backwards through a hedge and into a ditch. Jack stepped out unscathed, but perhaps just a little wiser.

In my mirrors I could see the Ferraris of Phil Hill and 'Taffy' Trips taking up the chase, but while the rain continued to fall - which it did spasmodically - I was able to hold a small but significant advantage. On the second lap Graham Hill shunted his BRM and Innes Ireland had to scramble out of his Lotus rather nippily since it had caught fire. Meanwhile, I was just able to hold the Ferraris at bay, although as time went on and the track dried my confidence ebbed. Of the Ring's 14 miles, some 12½ are made up of a succession of twists and turns. The one-and-a-half mile run-in to the start/finish, however, is dead straight and it was here that the Ferraris could catch up hand-over-fist. Each lap as I exited from the Döttinger Höhe right-hander leading on to the straight my eyes would be glued to the mirrors, waiting for the Ferraris to appear. I would count the seconds before the two red cars swept into view, praying that I had been able to hold my lead sufficiently. Once through the pit area I could breathe again. I would be able to look across after negotiating the South Curve U-turn to see exactly how far in front I was; usually the Ferraris would be rushing across the line while I prepared to plunge left-handed into the forest and the relative safety of a winding road.

I had been told by Dunlop, rather pessimistically, that after eight laps my D12s would burst - and the race was 15 laps! Luckily, there had been enough wet road to keep down the rate of wear, but as eight laps came and went, with von Trips now leading Hill (Mairesse had crashed on lap six) the road was virtually completely dry and my lead diminishing. For once, however, luck was on my side; just as it seemed von Trips would come charging past – at one point he was only six seconds behind – the rain returned. Over the final few laps I could see the red blobs in my mirrors become smaller and smaller and, despite the gloomy prognostications before the start, my tyres looked and felt OK. Little did I know that the rears had only 1 mm of tread left! I completed the course just over 20 seconds ahead of von Trips, with Hill third 1.1 seconds behind. Apparently the Ferraris almost hit each other during that final lap when they both slid on a puddle. Had they done so it might have been a clean sweep for the British, because Clark (Lotus) and Surtees (Cooper) occupied the next two places ahead of McLaren's Cooper and Ginther's Porsche.

While I was driving for Rob, I always found it pleasing to beat factory-entered cars, and it was most gratifying of all to beat the Ferraris. In '61, La Scuderia exercised a grip over Formula One racing such that they have not enjoyed since, even during the Niki Lauda era. They won five of the eight World Championship Grands Prix plus those F1 races at Syracuse and Naples. Indeed they contested no other events. Phil Hill won the World Drivers' Title at Monza and so the team didn't even bother to take part in the final Championship round at Watkins Glen, won by Ireland's works Lotus.

That I managed to 'do the dirty' on them just twice during that superlatively successful season stands vividly in my memory.

8 I race again

STIRLING MOSS

The idea of making a semi-serious return to the circuits had been lurking in the back of my mind for some time. During the latter part of the seventies I had accepted several drives in historic cars which I enjoyed very much indeed, but I realised that I could not be fully satisfied until I had taken things one step further. My main career in motor racing had lasted fourteen years and had been terminated prematurely. I knew in my heart of hearts that the old competitive urge was still bubbling away in my system and needed to be directed towards a more urgent and contemporary form of racing than historics. I felt that while single-seaters were out of the question, I might just be able to avoid making a fool of myself in some other form of modern racing car. I didn't want to launch myself into an area of high technology or sophistication, but at the same time I did want to compete on an equal footing with drivers of the modern era.

Saloon cars seemed the obvious choice and when, in the summer of 1979, Denny Hulme invited me to share a Volkswagen in a long-distance event in New Zealand, I accepted readily. I figured that in a race of this length (five and a half hours) I would have plenty of time to play myself in, while if I did make a hash of it, New Zealand was perhaps far enough away from Europe for none of my friends at home to notice!

For Denny, the race was very much a 'celebrity drive'. A New Zealander himself, he had won the World Championship in 1967 driving for Brabham, and had later been highly successful with the McLaren team, both in F1 and Can-Am. He had not retired until the end of 1974 and had no thoughts whatsoever of making a serious return to racing, although I know he still loves to have the odd go.

The car we were driving was a 1.6 litre VW Golf GTI. Because of the energy crisis the upper capacity limit for the race was restricted to 2,000cc so I could see we stood a real chance of outright victory. All the cars were in fairly standard form, rather as they are in the Tricentrol Championship in Britain, except that slick tyres were banned. The fact that ordinary road tyres were to be used actually helped me make up my mind to do the race. I had never raced on slicks and frankly I was wary of them; I was not sure, at that point, whether I would be able to alter my natural driving style to make full use of the vastly improved adhesion that such tyres offered.

In practice for the race – staged at the Pukekohe circuit and named the Benson and Hedges Production Saloon Car Classic – we qualified third fastest behind a Fiat 131R and another Golf GTI. The Fiat broke its diff. after a while, leaving Denny and I to chase the other VW. Unfortunately, while I was driving a front tyre blew and late in the race both the front wheels had to be changed a second time. In the end we lost by about 50 yards!

I had thoroughly enjoyed the experience and learnt some useful lessons. I now knew that I could still put up a reasonable show on a race track in a modern, if ordinary, kind of car and I discovered too that I still had the necessary stamina to keep up the pace for lap after lap; of the five and a half hours, I drove for three and felt fine.

I resolved straight away to try and fix myself a regular drive in a saloon during 1980. These days it seems that, no matter what category of racing one is in, a sponsor is the Number One requirement. Fortunately, Akai were already convinced of the publicity value afforded by motorsport and a deal was struck between Akai, Audi, GTI Engineering and me. Akai had already supported Richard Lloyd in the 1979 Tricentrol British Saloon Car Championship and were also backing Barry Sheene.

Richard (who was once Cliff Richard's publicity manager!) had for some time been a front runner in the Tricentrol series. His cars are prepared by his own company, GTI Engineering, at Silverstone and in 1979 he won the 1600cc class in a VW GTI basically similar to the one I had raced in New Zealand.

For 1980, however, he had decided to switch to Audi and in the Championship he and I were to race identical Audi 80 GLEs. The engine used in the Audi is virtually identical to the one in the VW Golf GTI so that clearly Richard and his men would feel at home with the power unit. Like the Golf, the Audi has front-wheel drive and a five-speed gearbox. Regulations for the Tricentrol Championship forbid much in the way of alteration to the basic engine, but by careful 'blueprinting' (matching parts to maker's tolerances so as to produce a so-called 'perfect' unit), by playing with the fuel injection and using an open exhaust the power output of the Audi went up from its standard 110 bhp to around the 140 bhp mark. With suitable gearing this gave an all-out maximum of about 130 mph.

I found the acceleration and overall speed of the car quite impressive. But the greatest difference between it and the road-going version lies in the slick tyres. In this series, slicks were allowed and so for the first time in my life I found myself driving on treadless rubber to experience cornering values which at first I just could not believe. Given also that, the New Zealand race apart, I had never raced a front-wheel drive car, I found I had a lot to learn. Even now as I write I don't think I have become fully used to the required driving technique. To start with, there is this fantastic roadholding; it's only a touring car, but I reckon the Audi, on slick tyres, has a cornering ability 15 per cent higher than the Formula One cars of the early sixties. However, being front-wheel drive, instead of the back end drifting out as one reaches the limit, the front end just runs wider and wider. Under racing circumstances I was not used to any of this and so I have been forced to change my natural method of driving quite appreciably.

Not that the car is difficult to drive. So many corners can be taken flat out that pure skill becomes less of a factor. However, I have found myself reaching my fear threshold earlier and I need more courage than perhaps I expected would be necessary. To keep cornering with your right foot screwed to the floor does take guts, but not always skill. Personally I would rather the car had more power, enough to make me lift off rather than keep the throttle wide open the whole time. On a 115 mph corner, for instance, I would prefer to go in at 116 mph then back off to 115 and take the corner than to stay at 115 all the time. The idea of slowing for corners, however slightly – it might not be more than lifting from the throttle and then immediately going hard down again – always gave me a feeling of security, of confidence, which sometimes I miss. Obviously I am older now which means perhaps that security becomes more important!

But because of the type of car that the Audi is, with its enormous roadholding, its inherent understeer and its relatively low power, I know I cannot drive it with as much finesse as I used to drive, say, the F1 Maserati 250F or the Vanwall. The degree of polish required in one's driving to get results is apparently very much smaller today, at least in saloon cars.

This type of racing quickly leads to frustration. There are four classes and I'm in the third fastest, so obviously I've had to become reconciled to being passed on the straight. The problem is that many Triumph Dolomites, for example, were easily faster in a straight line at Silverstone, but appreciably less rapid through the turns. The result was that I would go into a corner maybe 40 yards behind, then find I had to back off to avoid hitting them. For me that's very frustrating and I suppose the only answer is to move into a larger-engined class myself.

By the time anyone reads this the 1980 season will be over and I only hope that I will, by then, have more to shout about than I do right now. Talking now, after four races, I have yet to make it to the finish and naturally I am disappointed both for myself and my entrant. Everything was put together in a bit of a rush at the start of the season and reliability has certainly suffered through lack of testing.

Even so, I'm not unhappy in the way I've gone from a personal point of view. At the first meeting, at Mallory Park on March 23, I remember thinking, 'Boy, this is what it's all about!' There were two saloon races that day, one for the larger two classes and one for the smaller two. In practice I was hampered by a faulty rev counter, a puncture and an engine which ingested a stone. My 57.4 second practice lap was good enough only for sixth position and looked poor compared to the 54.2 time for Chris Hodgetts in his Toyota Celica. Still, there were another eleven cars behind me - including Richard who had suffered with a terrible misfire - and over the first couple of laps I was delighted to find I could outbrake one or two of the others into the hairpin.

I really felt quite at home, which boosted my confidence enormously. There was none of that 'fish out of water' feeling that deep down I had feared and that I'm sure a lot of people anticipated. Then, after four laps, the throttle linkage broke and that was that. I managed to set second fastest lap of the race (won by John Morris in a VW Scirocco) and certainly I had high hopes for the next two races over the Easter period. On Good Friday at Oulton Park I set fastest lap of the first practice at 1 minute 13.06 seconds, just quicker than Richard. I think Vic Elford, the team manager, rather wanted me to settle for that time in the second session. My view was that why should I make do with a four-minute mile when I could try for three minutes fifty? I didn't go quicker, as it happened, partly through having the wrong axle ratio for the circuit, but I've never felt that a practice time was unbeatable, no matter how early I might have established it, and I have no intention of changing my attitude now. I made a poor start at Oulton, pulled back to fourth but then found the clutch was slipping. A distributor gasket had failed, allowing oil to seep down on to the clutch. I struggled on to finish ninth.

A day later at Thruxton - a circuit I'd never raced on before - I practised fourth fastest in the class, but with Richard sidelined with a blown rocker gasket I could see that reliability was still the major worry. On race day, Easter Monday, I managed to compete at two circuits! I was entered for the historic meeting at Silverstone as well as in the Audi at Thruxton, but fortunately the timing was such that I was able to commute between the two circuits fast enough to do both. After practising Anthony Bamford's beautiful Ferrari Dino 246 at Silverstone in the morning, I was whisked by helicopter to Thruxton for the Tricentrol race. Immediately after that, the helicopter flew me straight back to Silverstone where my race was the last on the programme. In the Audi I soon became embroiled in a dust-up with Hodgetts, Morris and Richard

Longman's Ford Fiesta and by lap four I was lying second in the class with the car going well. Then the throttle broke again and, after that had been fixed in the pits, the clutch went just as it had at Oulton. This really was a bit much and I was in something of a depressed mood as I took off for Silverstone. After all my troubles, it is nice to record that the Ferrari went like a dream to finish first, just ahead of its 'twin' driven by Willie Green!

The old stigma of 'car breaker' was beginning to stir itself and as I write I'm still worried that those not immediately concerned with the team might prefer to blame me rather than the car for lack of results. There's only one thing worse in motor racing than continually failing to finish, and that's when you are unfairly accused of somehow ruining the car. It happened to me 20 years ago and I dread the thought of a recurrence today.

Testing between Thruxton and the next race, the International Trophy meeting at Silverstone, had resulted in more throttle failures and since vibration was the suspected culprit much stronger cables had been fitted. Understeer was the big problem in practice and on his home circuit Richard was two seconds a lap quicker than I was. I fancied that I might be able to keep with him in the race, but the old problem of baulking soon raised its head. I became mixed up in a battle between Tony Lanfranchi and Derrick Brunt in Vauxhall Magnums, Roger Saunders in a Dolomite and Morris's VW. The Vauxhalls and the 'Dolly' were in the class above and would outstrip me on the straights, only to get in the way at each corner. Things got quite hairy at times and I was just trying to work out a way to get rid of them when the throttle broke yet again. I coasted to a halt between Abbey and the Chicane and was able to enjoy a first-hand view of one of the Magnums turning turtle right at the end of the race to finish upside down in the middle of the track with the marshals panicking like mad. The event was actually stopped because of this two laps early, although the driver was safe and there was plenty of road either side of the car.

Whereas in my day saloon car events were contested in a fairly gentlemanly fashion, with most drivers having a go for sheer fun, today the 'professional' attitude which prevails has created a very cut-and-thrust approach. There's a lot more pushing and shoving than I was used to. Such a code of ethics which I might have adhered to in the fifties, and which I would have expected my rivals to observe, has all but disappeared. I have had to get used to being 'chopped' mercilessly going into corners. In the old days, we would usually have allowed the other man just enough room to get round on his own line - either that or pass him far enough before the corner so as to move over without carving him up. Today, the art of 'shutting the gate', or deliberately blocking a legitimate overtaking manoeuvre by cutting across one's bows, seems to be standard practice. I would hope to avoid employing such tactics myself, but clearly there is a limit to the amount one can take without retaliating.

It could be that the racing becomes more 'ethical' as one moves up a class or two - although watching the way they drive in Grand Prix races I'm not so sure! Assuming things work out well in 1980 I would certainly aim at competing in the top saloon category, currently limited to cars up to 3,500cc. This would pitch me in with the Capris and the Rovers and I would like to think the extra power would suit my style. Obviously a lot depends on what Akai intend to do. I'm still playing myself in and since, in my first four races, I've only completed something like twelve laps it really is a bit early to speculate on exactly how successful I'm likely to be. However, if things pick up I would certainly hope to continue for quite a few years yet and that would obviously mean bigger and more powerful cars. I don't anticipate any form of single-seater racing, other than historics, but until I feel completely happy racing on modern day tyres I can't honestly say where I'll draw the line.

I'm racing today because I like to, not because I have to and so the incentives are different. I take the actual business of racing *almost* as seriously as I used to because I believe if a thing's worth doing it's worth doing properly. Everyone concerned with the car at GTI Engineering, and at Audi themselves, put in an enormous amount of effort and it's down to me to try as hard as them. To be successful in racing no member of the organisation can afford to take things lightly, least of all the driver. On the other hand, I'm only in saloon car racing not Formula One, and so the requirements are that much less rigid. My own preparation is perhaps not quite as stringent as it was when I was racing for Vanwall although I still don't smoke and I drink very little. But after all, if I am competing for pleasure, I might as well have all the fun I can.

9 Bikes — my two greatest years

MIKE HAILWOOD

It may seem an odd thing to say but the two seasons of motorcycle racing in which I rode best of all were those in which I did *not* win the 500cc World Championship.

The years were 1966 and 1967 - ones in which, ironically, I abandoned car racing so as to concentrate on bikes in an effort to win the world title for Honda. I had managed to win four consecutive 500cc Championships for MV-Agusta, but switching to the new 4-cylinder Honda in '66 presented a new challenge. Honda were also contesting the 250cc and 350cc classes so for the first time there was a chance that I could capture three titles in a single season - something no rider had done then (or has even now!). Giacomo Agostini, runner-up in the 500cc category in 1965, was to lead the MV team and my team-mate Jim Redman and I looked forward to some tough battles. We were not to be disappointed!

South African Redman had ridden very successfully for Honda for several seasons. He had won the 250cc title in 1962 and 1963 and the 350cc Championship in the years 1962-65 inclusive. When the team entered the top 500cc category in 1966, he was naturally chosen as Number One rider. We agreed that I was to try and win the 250 and 350 Championships, while Jim should have a go at the 500 title. In motorcycle racing each capacity class has its own World Championship, from 50cc right up to 500cc, and sidecars on top of that. But, while it was always very nice to be successful in the smaller classes, it's the 500cc category that has always counted for most. Stepping up from the 250 and 350 machines is a natural progression but not always an easy one to make successfully. Jim was taking such a step in 1966, and to start with all went well. He won the opening 500cc Grand Prix at Hockenheim, beating Agostini, while I won the 250 and 350 events. As team captain, Jim obviously had the pick of the 500cc bikes, but as it turned out there was only ever one decent machine anyway!

We got to Assen for the Dutch Grand Prix and I didn't have one point – nor did I feel I stood much chance of gaining any. My 500 was a bit of a hotchpotch and to make matters worse I made a very bad start, which annoyed me so much I decided to give it a real go. I set out after the leaders, who naturally enough were Agostini and Redman. I was riding flat out, determined not to let this rather difficult Honda get the better of me. I passed Jim and I passed Ago and I thought, 'Great, I can win this to make it three victories in one day'. I had already been successful in the 250cc and 350cc events and a hat-trick would have been just what the doctor ordered. Unfortunately, no sooner had I established a lead than I fell off on my backside! The gearbox seemed to have a lot more neutrals in it than gears and on one corner I had managed to select a neutral instead of a cog and off I came. Jim sailed on to win the race, with Ago second.

In the very next race, the Belgian Grand Prix at Spa, Jim fell off and broke his arm. This was the race when it poured with rain while I was leading and I packed it in after Redman had crashed, allowing Agostini to chalk up his first victory of the year. Jim's injury was quite a nasty one and effectively dashed his hopes of carrying off the title. In fact, he decided to retire from racing altogether, which left me alone to chase Agostini. By the time we arrived in Brno for what, I think, was the fifth round of the Championship, the Czechoslovakian Grand Prix, he had amassed twenty-seven points while I still had nothing at all to show for my efforts. It was galling because I was well on my way to victory in the 250cc and 350cc Championships. To stand any chance of all three titles, I knew I needed all the luck in the world over the second half of the season.

I won in Brno, with Ago second, but he reversed the order in the Finnish Grand Prix at Imatra. I then beat him in the Ulster Grand Prix at Dundrod and again in the Isle of Man TT, but, of course, by continually finishing second he was still able to pile up the points. Unfortunately for him, the scoring system allowed only the best five results to be counted from the nine races that year, so as we went into the final round at Monza, Ago could claim only 36 points from his real total of 48, while I could keep all my points, which added up to 33. Moreover, since I had scored in four races only, whatever I did in Italy would also be allowed to count in full. Ago, on the other hand, already had two wins and five second places to his credit, so that only a victory at Monza could improve his Championship score. The points were awarded 9-6-4-3-2-1 from first place to sixth, so to overtake Ago I had to finish in the first three. What it boiled down to was whichever one of us won the race would be the World Champion, so naturally I was well wound up at the start.

I set off as hard as I could and built up a substantial lead. Agostini was lying second, as ever, but I was miles in front and beginning to count my chickens when, three laps from the end, the gearbox stuck in neutral. My race ended there and then, leaving me to watch Ago sweep home to take both the Grand Prix and the title. That was a bitter blow because I did feel I had ridden as well that year as at any time. I had, as planned, managed to carry off the 250 and 350 Championships, but frankly they were poor consolation for failing to capture the major prize.

But if 1966 had been a cliffhanger, it was nothing compared with the tension that lasted all through the following season! Again, it was a question of myself on the Honda versus Ago on the MV-Agusta. Unfortunately, the Honda was never quite as reliable as the MV and this, combined with Agostini's unflappable consistency, was to cost me dear.

There were ten 500cc Grands Prix that year, and he and I were to win five apiece. Ago won the opening round at Hockenheim, but I got my revenge by winning the TT. I remember dicing with him hard during that race, both of us going as fast as we dared. As we set off on the penultimate lap I had just a one second advantage – that's how close it was. Then the chain broke on the MV to destroy Ago's chances.

At Assen in Holland I beat him into second place, but he promptly turned the tables at Spa, where the Honda proved as big a pig as it had ever been. Ago won again in the East German Grand Prix at the Sachsenring while I retired, and although I captured the Czechoslovakian round, Ago was there in second place to go six points ahead. In Finland he triumphed for a fourth time, while I fell off. This gave him a total of 48 points compared to my 33 with just three rounds to go.

Happily, I scored maximum points in the Ulster Grand Prix, where it was Ago's turn to be left with nothing (I believe his clutch let him down). This made the score 48-42 with two rounds left, each of us having won four races. I had one second place to my credit but Ago had two – and this was to prove crucial.

For once the Italian Grand Prix at Monza was not to be the final round, as this year the Canadians were running an end-of-season GP at Mosport. But again I felt that whichever of us won at Monza would very likely be the 1967 Champion and so once more I just went as fast as I could from the flagfall. The similarity between this and the previous year's race was uncanny. I had half a lap lead over Ago and was just trying to work out what sort of advantage I would have in the points table when the gearbox played up just two laps from the end. Agostini passed me to win at a record speed of 124.37 mph, or just over 200 kph, the first time the magic figure had been achieved at Monza. I struggled on to finish second but, failing an Agostini blowup in Canada, the title was his.

That year, with a total of 10 Championship rounds, each rider was allowed to count his best six scores (half the number of races plus one). If the result was a tie then the Championship would be decided on the most wins, then the most second places, etc. If the tally was still level, the best seven placings would be considered, then the best eight and so on. After Italy I had 48 points from six results and Ago had 51 points from his best six, but with an additional second place 'up his sleeve'. I had won four events to his five and had finished second twice.

The situation as I understood it – and it was complicated – was this. It was still theoretically possible for me to share the title, but to do so I would not only have to win at Mosport, but hope that somehow Ago would fail to finish in the first six! If I did win, this would give me a total of 51 points – five wins and one second place to count (I would have to drop my second place points from Monza). If Ago finished out of the points in Canada, he would also have 51 points from five victories and a second place, plus a dropped second place. We would neither of us have any other results to call upon, so the Championship would thus have been tied.

As it was I did win the race, but to no great avail; that man Agostini was there in second place just as I had expected. He could thus count two 'extra' second places to my one. It had, without doubt, been the closest-fought Championship of all time. It was ironic that my gearbox should have let me down two years in succession at the same circuit and virtually at the same point – and both times it cost me the 500 title. However, 'ifs' and 'buts' have no real place in motorsport, and the fact was that whichever way you looked at it, Agostini had been more successful over those two seasons than I had. His era on top was just beginning while mine, clearly, was at an end. When Honda pulled out of motorcycle racing at the end of 1967 I gradually slipped back into the clutches of car racing, while Ago went on to win six more 500cc Championships.

I had ridden all I knew during those two years and I think I can honestly say that, when the Honda was performing as it should, I could get away from anyone. You can't knock Ago's determination, though, not to mention the superb reliability of the MV. Perhaps if I had not switched from the Italian team, things would have been different. On the other hand, I would hate to have missed the experience of taming that big Honda.

10 Motorcycle heroes past and present

MIKE HAILWOOD

I was privileged during my motorcycle racing career to compete against some of the hardest and fastest riders the sport has ever seen. It's virtually impossible to compare individual riders of different eras, but I do believe that the top men I raced against were a match for any of the 'greats' of today. Many, like Geoff Duke, Giacomo Agostini and Phil Read, won numerous Grand Prix races and became famous names. Others, through bad luck or bad management, failed to get into the limelight on an international scale, yet were nevertheless always tough competitors of the highest ability.

My choice for the greatest of the lot may come as a surprise to many people. He's a man who never became a World Champion, indeed he never so much as won a 500cc Grand Prix. But for my money, out of all the names one could conjure with – Duke, Ago, Bob McIntyre, Alistair King, Jim Redman, Gary Hocking and so on – the one that stands out as being the hardest of all to beat was a guy called Derek Minter.

Those new to motorcycle racing may never even have heard of Derek. But British fans of the early sixties will need no reminding of how he won race after race at Brands Hatch and Oulton Park. He was also outstanding on the Isle of Man and in 1962 he won the 250cc TT, beating Redman who became Champion that year. I've thought about it a lot over the past few years and I'm convinced that Derek was, on any circuit and at any time, the toughest competitor that I faced. He was called the 'King of Brands' and, on UK circuits in particular, he was very, very quick indeed. He didn't do a lot of international races, but when he did he was still a considerable force to be reckoned with. For instance, I recall him giving me a very hard time in the Dutch Grand Prix in 1962. I was on the 4-cylinder

MV-Agusta while almost everyone else, including Derek, was riding single-cylinder Nortons. The MV had a distinct power advantage but Minter went like a demon and I had to really fight to stay ahead. Eventually he finished in second place, ahead of Phil Read's similar machine.

Quite why Derek never made it into a works team remains something of a mystery. I can only assume it was because he had the wrong image. He had a way about him which meant that whenever he opened his mouth he tended to put his foot in it. Derek knew he was good, and he would never shrink from telling you as much, which naturally annoyed a lot of people. But in fact he was even better than he himself claimed! What made him such an awkward proposition, though, was that he would never admit defeat. For most riders there was, and is, a great tendency to 'play oneself in' over the first couple of laps. Minter would have none of this, he was flat out from the start. If you did manage to pass him somewhere, which wasn't likely, he would always have another go back and would probably get by you again. I know that, more often than not, he would beat me, given machines of roughly equal performance. After all these years I can't be certain, but I do feel that he won more races against me than I won against him.

Others will disagree with me about Minter. 'What about Surtees?' they may ask, 'What about Roberts?' The answer is that I never rode against these men - not on an equal footing, at least - and I can only realistically comment on those riders with whom I used to race regularly. Mark you, there were plenty who were almost as tough as Derek. Bob McIntyre was most definitely one. Unlike Derek, who was never properly recognised for the talent he possessed, Bob exuded real charisma. He became the first man to lap the Isle of Man course at over 100 mph, which turned him into a legendary figure, and he had a huge popular following. He did have a few lucky breaks, though. In 1957 he was drafted into the works Gilera team but only, I think, because Geoff Duke had fallen off and broken his arm. He finished second in the 500cc Championship that year to another Gilera man, Italian Libero Liberati, and was thereafter regarded as quite a star. But although he was always a hard rider, he was hard on machinery as well. More often than not, his bikes would blow up. It was always put down to 'Bob Mac's bad luck,' but as with the New Zealand racing driver Chris Amon, who never won a Championship F1 Grand Prix despite years at the top, you can only take 'bad luck' so far.

Despite his popularity, Bob was cast very much in the role of the dour Scot. It took a long time for me to get to know him but often by coincidence we used to finish up in the same hotels during the short circuit season and the night before a race we would as likely as not have a couple of jars together. He was a difficult character to understand but, as far as anyone knew him well, I think I probably did. When we raced against each other he was always extremely fair, very sporting. If I went by him at a hairpin or somewhere we'd always look at each other and have a smile or a laugh, or even pat each other on the back as we were going along!

Sadly, Bob was killed at Oulton Park, I think at the end of 1962, but he was always a marvellously good man to race against. Had he been just that little bit easier on his bikes he might well have been a World Champion.

There were hundreds in that category. Bob Anderson, who later turned to F1 car racing and was killed at Silverstone; Alan Trow, who also dabbled in single-seaters; John Hartle ... the list is almost endless. Hartle was indeed another who, on his day, was stunningly brilliant. But he used to work himself into such a frenzy that you could almost guarantee he would fall off. He used to go fast, very hard indeed, only to make a mistake somewhere. It was perhaps no great surprise when he finally got killed racing, although his was a tragic loss nevertheless.

Agostini, of course, was the man who in terms of sheer results gave me more trouble than anyone. Any rider who can win 15 World Championships - eight at 500cc and seven at 350cc - has got to be somebody very special indeed, and Ago was superb whenever he raced. Even so, looking back, I honestly don't believe I ever felt I could not beat him, given equal machinery, or possibly even something slightly inferior. By remaining faithful to MV until they pulled out of racing in 1975, Ago always had the best bike around, and he made the most of them. In the one season when we both had works MV-Agustas, 1965, he didn't beat me once, other than in Finland where I retired, and later Phil Read had the measure of him when he too joined the Italian team. But Ago has the enormous distinction of having been the man to beat virtually for a decade in motorcycle racing and if length of time at the top is the ultimate yardstick by which we may be judged, then he will very likely go down as the greatest biker of all time. Certainly part of the secret of his success lies in his genuine love of the sport. Ago enjoyed his bike racing with a passion, and even when he finally found himself being beaten by the 'new men' in the late seventies he could not bring himself to quit the tracks altogether. By switching to cars - he competes in the Aurora Formula One series with a Williams - he's still doing what he likes best. The odd thing is, although he seems to have been at it for generations, he's actually younger than me!

Whereas, having competed against them so often, I have fairly clear views on the riders of my era, I find it difficult to assess the relative merits of the modern-day racer. As a former rider everyone expects me to sum up today's men with a practised ease. But, short of actually racing with them, I can't see how I should be able to judge a rider's ability any more astutely than the next man. Obviously, one has to say that Kenny Roberts is, in 1980, head and shoulders above the rest. He's the complete professional, he gets the job done and he wins races. He's very fast, very consistent and very safe. He's got what is certainly the best bike and if he doesn't capture a third 500cc title to add to those of 1978 and 1979 I shall be very surprised.

Of the British riders, I will not hesitate to say that Ron Haslam is the best of what, frankly, isn't a terribly inspiring bunch. I think right now, in the summer of 1980, he's better even than Sheene (who is clearly going through a bad patch, trying to run his own team). Unfortunately, however, Haslam hasn't been exposed to much in the way of international, overseas competition, World Championship standard racing in other words. He's phenomenal at circuits like Brands, Mallory, Oulton and Donington and in the Transatlantic meeting of Easter 1980 he was the only one of the British team who looked remotely like giving the Americans a run for their money. But he desperately needs to get experience at Continental circuits like Assen, Imola, Spa and Jarama. Already he's left it a little bit late. If he had managed to break into the Grand Prix circus a couple of years ago, he might be a world class runner now. As it is, it might well be a case of unfulfilled potential. Winning a bunch of local races with all your fans cheering you on is all very well, but unless you at least get your foot in the door of World Championship racing you can hardly expect to progress much further.

Why Britain doesn't have more new stars on the horizon I'm not sure. The problem is that we seem to produce a string of promising riders like Haslam, Dave Potter, Roger Marshall, Keith Huewen and so on who hardly ever seem to travel further afield than their own backyards. Perhaps the state of the economy is to blame. If British sponsors fight shy of putting enough money in, then that leaves the way open to well-financed foreign teams. Certainly it seems to be the overseas competitor who can afford to travel from country to country, to go testing, to blow up a few bikes in an effort to discover the natural limits of both themselves and their machines. If you daren't ride to the limit because you can't afford a rebuild, nobody is ever going to know how good you are. It's a vicious circle.

At the so-called top level of motorcycle racing, I'd like to see British riders chancing their arms much more than they do. But to put it bluntly, the average good-class competitor today does not appear to me to ride anywhere near as hard as I and my contemporaries used to. On ordinary short circuits, we were on or close to what we felt was 'the limit' ninety per cent of the time. Now most of them *look* as though they've got quite a bit to spare. Of course, the limits are a lot higher today. The bikes have got more power than I was used to, and far greater adhesion. In my day, in fact, the winner was the guy who could get the furthest *over* the limit and get away with it. Watching modern racing, I get the impression that the limit is not even approached. I might be wrong, but I simply do not believe the majority of today's lads are sticking their necks out as much as we did.

There are exceptions to prove the theory. Over Easter 1980, the new American sensation Freddy Spencer (all of eighteen years old) slaughtered the opposition at Brands Hatch and went on to play the major role in his team's crushing victory over the British team (who had me as team manager, I'm ashamed to say!). He was riding after the style of ten or twenty years ago. He was giving it everything, it looked a bit dodgy and it was: but he got the results he wanted. We used to ride like that all the time - not just now and then, but regularly. I hate to get morbid about it, but why is it that so few racing motorcyclists are killed these days?

Fair enough, the helmets are better than they used to be and so are the circuits themselves. And, of course, I'm delighted the accident rate has fallen. I know only too well what it's like to be hurled down the road at very high speed and really it's only luck that has allowed me to survive until now. But even so the idea of riders of the eighties not giving quite as much of themselves as we did is disappointing to say the least. And it's an idea that recurs every time I see a motorcycle race.

As far as I can make out, and I am quite prepared to admit that Hailwood has probably got it all wrong yet again, the reason riders fall off nowadays is not because they are over the limit, but because they make simple, basic errors at high speed. They might misjudge their braking, or their line, or the road surface. But they don't come a cropper through trying too hard, that's for certain. Having raced modern bikes I can at least say positively that to reach the limit on a Suzuki RG500 or a Yamaha TZ500 I would have had to have gone a lot quicker than I did either on the Isle of Man or at the other events I took part in at Mallory and Donington. Even so, I was relatively successful against such opposition as I faced. Of course, I didn't race against Kenny Roberts or Virginio Ferrari or Randy Mamola or Barry Sheene. But in all honesty I *shouldn't* have been good enough, after ten years away from bikes, to win a couple of TTs. The fact that I did is, in a way, a curious indictment against the general standard of riding which exists at least in this country at the moment.

To me, bike racing has always been safer than car racing. I was prepared to go equally hard in both, but in cars I was always aware that a wheel might fall off, or that the suspension might break, or that the brakes would fail, or the aerodynamics go awry, and that when it did crash it would catch fire with me inside, trapped by a six-point safety harness. Bikes don't fail in that manner, and if they do catch fire you can be sure the rider is well away from the machine. Mercifully, the danger of fire in a car accident has been radically reduced since I was racing, but I still maintain that four wheels are inherently more dangerous than two. Having said that, I have to acknowledge that both forms of motorsport involve calculated risks. And it is crystal clear to me that to win a race, whether it's in a car or on a bike, one has to take those risks. Not just to accept them, but indulge in them. It's the same whether you are playing tiddlywinks, or cards, or any game involving a degree of chance. In bike racing you are in the 'risk business' up to your neck and sometimes beyond, so let's not disguise the fact. I accept, and all those taking part must accept, that the consequences of taking risks on a bike in a race can be horrendous. Then again, nobody *has* to do it; but if they do they might as well have a real go. Otherwise there's surely no point.

I've no doubt that the top few men in Grand Prix racing *do* take the kind of necessary risks that lead to the winner's rostrum. Men like Roberts, fellow Americans Randy Mamola and Mike Baldwin, Spencer of course, Virginio Ferrari of Italy and Dutchmen Wil Hartog and Boet van Dulman. The new Suzuki man, New Zealander Graeme Crosby, is another who, I think, knows he's got to get going fairly mightily if he's to emulate his predecessor, B. Sheene Esq. I've always been impressed by Graeme because I used to watch him race down under. When he decided to try his luck in Europe he asked me if I would give him a letter of recommendation, which I did. I sort of suggested that race meetings would benefit by his presence, that the guy was the greatest thing since sliced bread, modest stuff like that, in the hope that it would raise a little start money for him. This was back in '78 but almost straight away 'Croz' finished fourth in the Formula 1 (Production) TT on a sit-up-and-beg Kawasaki. He went really well over the rest of the '79 season on four-stroke Formula 1 machinery and immediately secured a contract with Suzuki to race their Grand Prix two-stroke 500s during 1980. He's still got a lot to learn with regard both to the bike and the different circuits, but I'd like to see him come through with flying colours. His team-mate, Randy Mamola, was the sensation of 1979 and is another who could, in time, give Roberts big problems in the Championship. He's a no-nonsense, rugged competitor who took to European Grand Prix racing like a duck to water. He's only 20 years old but already he's got a year of top flight international racing behind him. And already, too, he has been superseded by Freddy Spencer as the youngest competitor in big-time racing! It really is amazing how every year the Americans seem to produce someone new. Over the past few years we've had Roberts, Stevie Baker, Pat Hennen, who unhappily crashed on the Island in 1978 and has not raced since, Skip Aksland, Mike Baldwin, and now Mamola and Spencer. No wonder our boys are not getting much of a look in.

Still, I do sometimes wonder whether all these brave blokes really are better than we were, or whether we were simply fooling ourselves. The bikes have improved so much I have no hesitation in saying that the degree of courage necessary to get the most out of them is greater than it used to be. On the other hand, I'm sure that it's a lot easier now to get to a certain standard in bike racing simply because the machines have themselves become more sophisticated, easier to control. To an extent, you *can* take greater liberties with them than I was able to take with the MV or the Honda. But because the things are so very powerful, I do estimate that, while the necessity to ride as near to the limit as possible remains the same, you have to be a very special kind of lunatic nowadays to do so! And I know for certain that I am profoundly happy it is them and not me out there right now.

Appendix: Racing careers

STIRLING MOSS

Formula One career record

*denotes World Championship Formula Two races. All World Championship rounds 1952-3 run to Formula Two rules.

Event	*Circuit*	*Car*	*Result*
1950			
Bari Grand Prix	Bari	HWM	3rd
International Trophy	Silverstone	HWM	6th
1951			
International Trophy	Silverstone	HWM	14th
Swiss Grand Prix	Bremgarten	HWM	8th
Dutch Grand Prix	Zandvoort	HWM	3rd
1952			
*Swiss Grand Prix	Bremgarten	HWM	Retired
Ulster Trophy	Dundrod	BRM V16	Retired
*Belgian Grand Prix	Spa-Francorchamps	ERA G-Type	Retired
*British Grand Prix	Silverstone	ERA G-Type	Retired
*Dutch Grand Prix	Zandvoort	ERA G-Type	Retired
*Italian Grand Prix	Monza	Connaught	Retired
1953			
*Dutch Grand Prix	Zandvoort	Connaught	9th
Rouen Grand Prix	Rouen	Cooper-Alta	Retired
*French Grand Prix	Reims	Cooper-Alta	Retired
*German Grand Prix	Nurburgring	Cooper-Alta	6th
*Italian Grand Prix	Monza	Cooper-Alta	13th
1954			
Bordeaux Grand Prix	Bordeaux	Maserati 250F	4th
International Trophy	Silverstone	Maserati 250F	Retired
Aintree 200	Aintree	Maserati 250F	1st
Rome Grand Prix	Castelfusano	Maserati 250F	6th
Belgian Grand Prix	Spa-Francorchamps	Maserati 250F	3rd
British Grand Prix	Silverstone	Maserati 250F	Retired
Caen Grand Prix	Circuit de la Prairie	Maserati 250F	2nd
German Grand Prix	Nurburgring	Maserati 250F	Retired

Gold Cup	Oulton Park	Maserati 250F	1st
Pescara Grand Prix	Pescara	Maserati 250F	Retired
Swiss Grand Prix	Bremgarten	Maserati 250F	Retired
Italian Grand Prix	Monza	Maserati 250F	10th
Goodwood Trophy	Goodwood	Maserati 250F	1st
Daily Telegraph Trophy	Aintree	Maserati 250F	1st
Spanish Grand Prix	Pedralbes	Maserati 250F	Retired
1955			
Argentine Grand Prix	Buenos Aires	Mercedes-Benz W196	4th
Glover Trophy	Goodwood	Maserati 250F	Retired
Bordeaux Grand Prix	Bordeaux	Maserati 250F	4th
International Trophy	Silverstone	Maserati 250F	Retired
Monaco Grand Prix	Monte Carlo	Mercedes-Benz W196	9th
Belgian Grand Prix	Spa-Francorchamps	Mercedes-Benz W196	2nd
Dutch Grand Prix	Zandvoort	Mercedes-Benz W196	2nd
British Grand Prix	Aintree	Mercedes-Benz W196	1st
Redex Trophy	Snetterton	Maserati 250F	3rd
Daily Telegraph Trophy	Aintree	Maserati 250F	Retired
Italian Grand Prix	Monza	Mercedes-Benz W196	Retired
Gold Cup	Oulton Park	Maserati 250F	1st
1956			
Argentine Grand Prix	Buenos Aires	Maserati 250F	Retired
Buenos Aires Grand Prix	Mendoza	Maserati 250F	2nd
Glover Trophy	Goodwood	Maserati 250F	1st
Aintree 200	Aintree	Maserati 250F	1st
International Trophy	Silverstone	Vanwall	1st
Monaco Grand Prix	Monte Carlo	Maserati 250F	1st
Belgian Grand Prix	Spa-Francorchamps	Maserati 250F	3rd
French Grand Prix	Reims	Maserati 250F	5th
British Grand Prix	Silverstone	Maserati 250F	Retired
German Grand Prix	Nurburgring	Maserati 250F	2nd
Italian Grand Prix	Monza	Maserati 250F	1st
1957			
Argentine Grand Prix	Buenos Aires	Maserati 250F	8th
Buenos Aires Grand Prix	Buenos Aires	Maserati 250F	6th
Syracuse Grand Prix	Syracuse	Vanwall	3rd
Glover Trophy	Goodwood	Vanwall	Retired
Monaco Grand Prix	Monte Carlo	Vanwall	Retired
British Grand Prix	Aintree	Vanwall	1st
German Grand Prix	Nurburgring	Vanwall	5th
Pescara Grand Prix	Pescara	Vanwall	1st
Italian Grand Prix	Monza	Vanwall	1st
1958			
Argentine Grand Prix	Buenos Aires	Cooper-Climax T45	1st
Glover Trophy	Goodwood	Cooper-Climax T45	Retired
Aintree 200	Aintree	Cooper-Climax T45	1st

International Trophy	Silverstone	Cooper-Climax T45	Retired
Monaco Grand Prix	Monte Carlo	Vanwall	Retired
Dutch Grand Prix	Zandvoort	Vanwall	1st
Belgian Grand Prix	Spa-Francorchamps	Vanwall	Retired
French Grand Prix	Reims	Vanwall	2nd
British Grand Prix	Silverstone	Vanwall	Retired
Caen Grand Prix	Circuit de la Prairie	Cooper-Climax T45	1st
German Grand Prix	Nurburgring	Vanwall	Retired
Portuguese Grand Prix	Oporto	Vanwall	1st
Italian Grand Prix	Monza	Vanwall	Retired
Moroccan Grand Prix	Ain-Diab	Vanwall	1st
1959			
Glover Trophy	Goodwood	Cooper-Climax T51	1st
Aintree 200	Aintree	Cooper-BRM T51	Retired
International Trophy	Silverstone	BRM P25	Retired
Monaco Grand Prix	Monte Carlo	Cooper-Climax T51	Retired
Dutch Grand Prix	Zandvoort	Cooper-Climax T51	Retired
French Grand Prix	Reims	BRM P25	8th
British Grand Prix	Aintree	BRM P25	2nd
German Grand Prix	Avus	Cooper-Climax T51	Retired
Portuguese Grand Prix	Monsanto	Cooper-Climax T51	1st
Italian Grand Prix	Monza	Cooper-Climax T51	1st
Gold Cup	Oulton Park	Cooper-Climax T51	1st
United States Grand Prix	Sebring	Cooper-Climax T51	Retired
1960			
Argentine Grand Prix	Buenos Aires	Cooper-Climax T51	3rd
Glover Trophy	Goodwood	Cooper-Climax T51	2nd
International Trophy	Silverstone	Cooper-Climax T51	Retired
Monaco Grand Prix	Monte Carlo	Lotus-Climax 18	1st
Dutch Grand Prix	Zandvoort	Lotus-Climax 18	4th
Belgian Grand Prix	Spa-Francorchamps	Lotus-Climax 18	Crashed in pract
Portuguese Grand Prix	Oporto	Lotus-Climax 18	Retired
Gold Cup	Oulton Park	Lotus-Climax 18	1st
United States Grand Prix	Riverside	Lotus-Climax 18	1st
1961			
Glover Trophy	Goodwood	Lotus-Climax 18	4th
Brussels Grand Prix	Heysel	Lotus-Climax 18	7th
Vienna Grand Prix	Aspern	Lotus-Climax 18	1st
Aintree 200	Aintree	Cooper-Climax T53	Retired
Syracuse Grand Prix	Syracuse	Lotus-Climax 18	8th
Monaco Grand Prix	Monte Carlo	Lotus-Climax 18	1st
Dutch Grand Prix	Zandvoort	Lotus-Climax 18	4th
Silver City Trophy	Brands Hatch	Lotus-Climax 18/21	1st
Belgian Grand Prix	Spa-Francorchamps	Lotus-Climax 18/21	8th
French Grand Prix	Reims	Lotus-Climax 18/21	Retired
British Grand Prix	Aintree	Lotus-Climax 18/21	Retired

Solitude Grand Prix	Solitude	Lotus-Climax 18/21	Retired
German Grand Prix	Nurburgring	Lotus-Climax 18/21	1st
Kanonloppet	Karlskoga	Lotus-Climax 18/21	1st
Danish Grand Prix	Roskildering	Lotus-Climax 18/21	1st
Modena Grand Prix	Modena	Lotus-Climax 18/21	1st
Italian Grand Prix	Monza	Lotus-Climax 21	Retired
Gold Cup	Oulton Park	Ferguson-Climax P99	1st
United States Grand Prix	Watkins Glen	Lotus-Climax 18/21	Retired
Natal Grand Prix	Westmead	Lotus-Climax 18/21	2nd
South African Grand Prix	East London	Lotus-Climax 18/21	2nd
1962			
Brussels Grand Prix	Heysel	Lotus-Climax 18/21V8	Retired
Lombank Trophy	Snetterton	Lotus-Climax 18/21 V8	7th
Glover Trophy	Goodwood	Lotus-Climax 18/21 V8	Retired

MIKE HAILWOOD

Motorcycle racing successes

In the period 1958-67 Mike Hailwood competed regularly in 250cc, 350cc and 500cc categories of the motorçycle World Championship and also, early on, in the 125cc class. So many races were involved that it would take several pages to mention them all. Below, however, is a list of Grand Prix victories achieved during Mike's incredible career.

Event	*Circuit*	*Machine*
1959		
Ulster Grand Prix	Dundrod	Ducati 125
1961		
Isle of Man TT	Isle of Man	Honda 125
Isle of Man TT	Isle of Man	Honda 250
Dutch Grand Prix	Assen	Honda 250
East German Grand Prix	Sachsenring	Honda 250
Swedish Grand Prix	Kristianstad	Honda 250
Isle of Man TT	Isle of Man	Norton 500
Italian Grand Prix	Monza	MV-Agusta 500
1962		
Isle of Man TT	Isle of Man	MV-Agusta 350
Dutch Grand Prix	Assen	MV-Agusta 500
Belgian Grand Prix	Spa-Francorchamps	MV-Agusta 500
Ulster Grand Prix	Dundrod	MV-Agusta 500
East German Grand Prix	Sachsenring	MV-Agusta 500
Italian Grand Prix	Monza	MV-Agusta 500

1963		
East German Grand Prix	Sachsenring	MZ 250
East German Grand Prix	Sachsenring	MV-Agusta 350
Finnish Grand Prix	Tampere	MV-Agusta 350
Isle of Man TT	Isle of Man	MV-Agusta 500
Belgian Grand Prix	Spa-Francorchamps	MV-Agusta 500
Ulster Grand Prix	Dundrod	MV-Agusta 500
East German Grand Prix	Sachsenring	MV-Agusta 500
Finnish Grand Prix	Tampere	MV-Agusta 500
Italian Grand Prix	Monza	MV-Agusta 500
Argentine Grand Prix	Buenos Aires	MV-Agusta 500
1964		
United States Grand Prix	Daytona	MV-Agusta 500
Isle of Man TT	Isle of Man	MV-Agusta 500
Dutch Grand Prix	Assen	MV-Agusta 500
Belgian Grand Prix	Spa Francorchamps	MV-Agusta 500
German Grand Prix	Solitude	MV-Agusta 500
East German Grand Prix	Sachsenring	MV-Agusta 500
Italian Grand Prix	Monza	MV-Agusta 500
1965		
Japanese Grand Prix	Suzuka	Honda 250
Japanese Grand Prix	Suzuka	Honda 350
United States Grand Prix	Daytona	MV-Agusta 500
German Grand Prix	Nurburgring	MV-Agusta 500
Isle of Man TT	Isle of Man	MV-Agusta 500
Dutch Grand Prix	Assen	MV-Agusta 500
Belgian Grand Prix	Spa-Francorchamps	MV-Agusta 500
East German Grand Prix	Sachsenring	MV-Agusta 500
Czechoslovakian Grand Prix	Brno	MV-Agusta 500
Italian Grand Prix	Monza	MV-Agusta 500
1966		
Spanish Grand Prix	Barcelona	Honda 250
German Grand Prix	Hockenheim	Honda 250
French Grand Prix	Clermont-Ferrand	Honda 250
Isle of Man TT	Isle of Man	Honda 250
Dutch Grand Prix	Assen	Honda 250
Belgian Grand Prix	Spa-Francorchamps	Honda 250
East German Grand Prix	Sachsenring	Honda 250
Czechoslovakian Grand Prix	Brno	Honda 250
Finnish Grand Prix	Imatra	Honda 250
Italian Grand Prix	Monza	Honda 250
German Grand Prix	Hockenheim	Honda 350
French Grand Prix	Clermont-Ferrand	Honda 350
Dutch Grand Prix	Assen	Honda 350
Czechoslovakian Grand Prix	Brno	Honda 350
Finnish Grand Prix	Imatra	Honda 350

Ulster Grand Prix	Dundrod	Honda 350
Czechoslovakian Grand Prix	Brno	Honda 500
Isle of Man TT	Isle of Man	Honda 500
Ulster Grand Prix	Dundrod	Honda 500
1967		
Isle of Man TT	Isle of Man	Honda 250
Dutch Grand Prix	Assen	Honda 250
Finnish Grand Prix	Imatra	Honda 250
Ulster Grand Prix	Dundrod	Honda 250
Canadian Grand Prix	Mosport	Honda 250
German Grand Prix	Hockenheim	Honda 350
Isle of Man TT	Isle of Man	Honda 350
Dutch Grand Prix	Assen	Honda 350
East German Grand Prix	Sachsenring	Honda 350
Czechoslovakian Grand Prix	Brno	Honda 350
Japanese Grand Prix	Fisco	Honda 350
Isle of Man TT	Isle of Man	Honda 500
Dutch Grand Prix	Assen	Honda 500
Czechoslovakian Grand Prix	Brno	Honda 500
Ulster Grand Prix	Dundrod	Honda 500
Canadian Grand Prix	Mosport	Honda 500

In 1978 Hailwood returned to the Isle of Man and won the Formula One Production TT on a Ducati. He returned in 1979 and won the Senior (500cc) TT on a Suzuki 500. By winning the Production TT he automatically became Formula One TT World Champion for 1978 since the title was to be decided on the one event only. The 1979 Senior TT, while being the greater success of the two, did not count towards the World Championship.

MIKE HAILWOOD

Formula One career record

Event	*Circuit*	*Car*	*Result*
1963			
British Grand Prix	Silverstone	Lotus-Climax 24	8th
Solitude Grand Prix	Solitude	Lola-Climax Mk 4	Not classified
Italian Grand Prix	Monza	Lola-Climax Mk 4	10th
Gold Cup	Oulton Park	Lola-Climax Mk 4	7th
1964			
Daily Mirror Trophy	Snetterton	Lotus-BRM 25	Retired

News of the World Trophy	Goodwood	Lotus-BRM 25	5th
Syracuse Grand Prix	Syracuse	Lotus-BRM 25	7th
Aintree 200	Aintree	Lotus-BRM 25	Retired
International Trophy	Silverstone	Lotus-BRM 25	6th
Monaco Grand Prix	Monte Carlo	Lotus-BRM 25	6th
Dutch Grand Prix	Zandvoort	Lotus-BRM 25	12th
French Grand Prix	Rouen	Lotus-BRM 25	8th
British Grand Prix	Brands Hatch	Lotus-BRM 25	Retired
Solitude Grand Prix	Solitude	Lotus-BRM 25	9th
German Grand Prix	Nurburgring	Lotus-BRM 25	Retired
Mediterranean Grand Prix	Pergusa	Lotus-BRM 25	Retired
Austrian Grand Prix	Zeltweg	Lotus-BRM 25	8th
Italian Grand Prix	Monza	Lotus-BRM 25	Retired
United States Grand Prix	Watkins Glen	Lotus-BRM 25	8th
Mexican Grand Prix	Mexico City	Lotus-BRM 25	Retired
1965			
Race of Champions	Brands Hatch	Lotus-BRM 25	Retired
Syracuse Grand Prix	Syracuse	Lotus-BRM 25	Retired
International Trophy	Silverstone	Lotus-BRM 25	9th
Monaco Grand Prix	Monte Carlo	Lotus-BRM 25	Retired
1971			
Italian Grand Prix	Monza	Surtees-Ford TS9	4th
United States Grand Prix	Watkins Glen	Surtees-Ford TS9	15th
Victory Race	Brands Hatch	Surtees-Ford TS9	Retired
1972			
South African Grand Prix	Kyalami	Surtees-Ford TS9B	Retired
Race of Champions	Brands Hatch	Surtees-Ford TS9B	2nd
International Trophy	Silverstone	Surtees-Ford TS9B	Retired
Spanish Grand Prix	Jarama	Surtees-Ford TS9B	Retired
Monaco Grand Prix	Monte Carlo	Surtees-Ford TS9B	Retired
Belgian Grand Prix	Nivelles	Surtees-Ford TS9B	4th
French Grand Prix	Clermont Ferrand	Surtees-Ford TS9B	6th
British Grand Prix	Brands Hatch	Surtees-Ford TS9B	Retired
German Grand Prix	Nurburgring	Surtees-Ford TS9B	Retired
Austrian Grand Prix	Osterreichring	Surtees-Ford TS9B	4th
Italian Grand Prix	Monza	Surtees-Ford TS9B	2nd
United States Grand Prix	Watkins Glen	Surtees-Ford TS9B	17th
John Player Victory Race	Brands Hatch	Surtees-Ford TS9B	9th
1973			
Argentine Grand Prix	Buenos Aires	Surtees-Ford TS14	Retired
Brazilian Grand Prix	Interlagos	Surtees-Ford TS14	Retired
South African Grand Prix	Kyalami	Surtees-Ford TS14	Retired
Race of Champions	Brands Hatch	Surtees-Ford TS14	Retired
International Trophy	Silverstone	Surtees-Ford TS14	Retired
Spanish Grand Prix	Montjuich Park	Surtees-Ford TS14	Retired
Belgian Grand Prix	Zolder	Surtees-Ford TS14	Retired

Monaco Grand Prix	Monte Carlo	Surtees-Ford TS14	8th
Swedish Grand Prix	Anderstorp	Surtees-Ford TS14	Retired
French Grand Prix	Clermont Ferrand	Surtees-Ford TS14	Retired
British Grand Prix	Silverstone	Surtees-Ford TS14	Retired
Dutch Grand Prix	Zandvoort	Surtees-Ford TS14	Retired
German Grand Prix	Nurburgring	Surtees-Ford TS14	14th
Austrian Grand Prix	Osterreichring	Surtees-Ford TS14	10th
Italian Grand Prix	Monza	Surtees-Ford TS14	7th
Canadian Grand Prix	Mosport	Surtees-Ford TS14	9th
United States Grand Prix	Watkins Glen	Surtees-Ford TS14	Retired
1974			
Argentine Grand Prix	Buenos Aires	McLaren-Ford M23	4th
Brazilian Grand Prix	Interlagos	McLaren-Ford M23	5th
Race of Champions	Brands Hatch	McLaren-Ford M23	4th
South African Grand Prix	Kyalami	McLaren-Ford M23	3rd
International Trophy	Silverstone	McLaren-Ford M23	Retired
Spanish Grand Prix	Jarama	McLaren-Ford M23	9th
Belgian Grand Prix	Nivelles	McLaren-Ford M23	7th
Monaco Grand Prix	Monte Carlo	McLaren-Ford M23	Retired
Swedish Grand Prix	Anderstorp	McLaren-Ford M23	Retired
Dutch Grand Prix	Zandvoort	McLaren-Ford M23	4th
French Grand Prix	Dijon	McLaren-Ford M23	7th
British Grand Prix	Brands Hatch	McLaren-Ford M23	Retired
German Grand Prix	Nurburgring	McLaren-Ford M23	Retired